Yorksh
Mount___ __bing
The South Dales

VERTEBRATE **GRAPHICS**
PUBLISHING

Design and production by Vertebrate Graphics Ltd, Sheffield
www.**v-graphics**.co.uk

Yorkshire Dales
MountainBiking

The South Dales

Written by
Nick Cotton

Yorkshire Dales
MountainBiking
The South Dales

VG Copyright © 2006 **Vertebrate Graphics Ltd**

VG Published by **Vertebrate Graphics Ltd**

ISBN 0-9548131-6-2

Cover photo: **Andy Heading**

Photography by **Andy Heading**
Additional photography **Nick Cotton**

Design by **Nathan Ryder** – Vertebrate Graphics Ltd.
Production by **Oliver Jackson** – Vertebrate Graphics Ltd.
Series editor **Tom Fenton** – Vertebrate Graphics Ltd.
www.**v-graphics**.co.uk

Vertebrate Graphics uses HARVEY mapping and map data.
Copyright 2006 HARVEY Maps. All rights reserved. No part
of this mapping may be reproduced without the written consent
of the copyright owner.

PLEASE GIVE WAY TO HORSES AND PEDESTRIANS.

Contents

ROUTE GRADES ▲ = MEDIUM ▲ = HARD ▲ = EXTREME (see page viii)

KEY TO THE MAP SYMBOLS

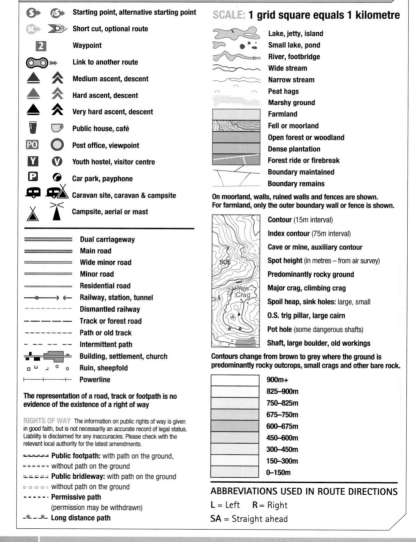

S➤ Starting point, **AS➤** alternative starting point

SC➤ Short cut, **OR➤** optional route

2 Waypoint

⬤➤ Link to another route

▲ Medium ascent, ⌃ descent

▲ Hard ascent, ⌃ descent

▲ Very hard ascent, ⌃ descent

🍺 Public house, ☕ café

PO Post office, ○ viewpoint

Y Youth hostel, ⓥ visitor centre

P Car park, **📞** payphone

🚐 Caravan site, 🚐 caravan & campsite

✕ Campsite, ✲ aerial or mast

═══════ Dual carriageway

═══════ Main road

──────── Wide minor road

──────── Minor road

──────── Residential road

──◇──→ ← Railway, station, tunnel

---------- Dismantled railway

── ── ── Track or forest road

--------- Path or old track

── -- ── -- Intermittent path

🏠 Building, settlement, church

▫ ⊔ ⅃ ° ○ Ruin, sheepfold

├──┼──┤ Powerline

The representation of a road, track or footpath is no evidence of the existence of a right of way.

RIGHTS OF WAY The information on public rights of way is given in good faith, but is not necessarily an accurate record of legal status. Liability is disclaimed for any inaccuracies. Please check with the relevant local authority for the latest amendments.

⌁⌁⌁⌁ **Public footpath:** with path on the ground,

----- without path on the ground

⌐⌐⌐⌐ **Public bridleway:** with path on the ground

○ ○ ○ ○ without path on the ground

- - - - - **Permissive path**

  (permission may be withdrawn)

⌁ - - ⌁ **Long distance path**

SCALE: 1 grid square equals 1 kilometre

Lake, jetty, island

Small lake, pond

River, footbridge

Wide stream

Narrow stream

Peat hags

Marshy ground

Farmland

Fell or moorland

Open forest or woodland

Dense plantation

Forest ride or firebreak

Boundary maintained

Boundary remains

On moorland, walls, ruined walls and fences are shown. For farmland, only the outer boundary wall or fence is shown.

Contour (15m interval)

Index contour (75m interval)

Cave or mine, auxiliary contour

505 Spot height (in metres – from air survey)

Predominantly rocky ground

Major crag, climbing crag

Spoil heap, sink holes: large, small

O.S. trig pillar, large cairn

Pot hole (some dangerous shafts)

Shaft, large boulder, old workings

Contours change from brown to grey where the ground is predominantly rocky outcrops, small crags and other bare rock.

	900m+
	825–900m
	750–825m
	675–750m
	600–675m
	450–600m
	300–450m
	150–300m
	0–150m

ABBREVIATIONS USED IN ROUTE DIRECTIONS

L = Left   **R** = Right

SA = Straight ahead

Introduction

The Yorkshire Dales offer the unique combination of an excellent network of stone-based bridleways, usable all year round, drop-dead gorgeous scenery rising to over 700m and, because of the spread-out nature of the trails, very little user conflict with either walkers or horseriders. Mountain-biking heaven on excellent trails weaving their way through a landscape of limestone plateaux, drystone walls, field barns, sheep pasture, clumps of broadleaf woodland, streams, rivers and waterfalls with fine pubs in almost all the villages from Kirkby Lonsdale in the west to Masham in the east.

Other highlights, among far too many to list in full, include classic trails such as Mastiles Lane between Kilnsey and Malham, the wonderful 'new' bridleways created by the National Park, where mud and chaos reigned before, over Gorbeck (west of Malham) and down from Weets Top (east of Malham), teeth-rattling descents down into Stainforth, and great swathes of heather-clad grouse moors criss-crossed by fine high level stone-based tracks, especially in the east in Nidderdale.

There is very little singletrack at all as most of the trails either use broad stone tracks at lower levels or broad grassy tracks higher up. Tracks to test you do not consist of a series of perfectly spaced drop-offs on a twisty woodland trail but lung-busting 250m climbs up steep stone tracks or loose stone descents where picking the right line has you crossing left to right across the path dodging the rubble traps.

The icing on the cake consists of long, cruising plateau sections on well-drained grass tracks or broad stone tracks over grouse moors which normally come as a reward for some horrendous climb and offer you the chance to sniff the breeze and open your eyes to the stupendous scenery that lies all around, an easy breather before the gradient steepens and you need to sharpen your wits for the downhill challenges.

Nick Cotton

Acknowledgements

Thanks to Mark Allum of the Yorkshire Dales National Park Authority for his support with the project, and the YDNPA itself for the great work it has done restoring many previously unrideable bridleways.

To Andy Heading, for his excellent photography, his input and suggestions and for his bike-dodging skills.

The VG team – Nathan Ryder and Oliver Jackson for their excellent design work, Tom Fenton for his editing and Jon Barton and Simon Norris for backing the projects and their work on earlier volumes which paved the way for this one.

Susan Harvey at Harvey Maps, for her help in providing mapping data.

Karen McDonald at Polaris for providing clothing for our photo sessions.

And to our photographic models, Andrew Whittaker, Ben Eagle, Pete Dodd, Jon Barton and Freya Bloor, for putting up with Andy's endless requests to "ride a little way back up that hill again".

How to use this book

The routes

We've tried to cover as many of the Dales' numerous trails as possible in this guide. The aim was to avoid bog trotting, to seek out the more 'interesting' sections and to take in any well-known bits that everybody should ride at some point in their lives. The routes we've come up with are just some of the vast number of ways of doing this. Try them as suggested, in reverse or joined to neighbouring routes. Once you've ridden a few and got to know the area a little, you'll be able to link your favourite sections of trail together into nice flowing rides where you don't need a map or guidebook at all.

Classics are generally fairly short (although not necessarily easy). **Epics** are a little longer and climb a little more. **Enduros** are a step up again, and the **Killers** are self-explanatory. We've also listed the pick of the area's descents and climbs in the **Bonus Section** on pages 180–191, which may help you choose your route.

Grades

We've graded the routes (and key climbs and descents) as Blue, Red or Black, in a similar system to that being adopted on several of the man-made trails around the UK.

This is roughly similar to the system used in skiing where:
▲ = Medium, ▲ = Hard and ▲ = Extreme.

These grades are based on summer conditions – little or no mud and, importantly, dry limestone. In a drought they might feel easier, in the depths of winter they will feel a little trickier and more slippery. They take into account technicality, length and remoteness. One 'black' ascent might be an all-out techno fest whilst another could be a drawn out endurance challenge.

As ever, these grades are subjective – even we disagreed when putting them in; how you find a given route, a specific downhill or a climb will be dictated by your personal levels of fitness, skill and bottle.

Maps, descriptions, distances

While every effort has been made to maintain accuracy within the maps and descriptions in this guide, things do change from time to time and we are unable to guarantee that every single detail is correct.

Please exercise caution if a direction appears at odds with the route on the ground. If in doubt, a comparison between the description and a map (along with a bit of common sense) should help ensure that you're on the right track.

Note that distances have been measured from the map and may not tally with a bike computer. Please treat stated distances as a guideline only.

Planning your ride

This book should provide you with all the information you need for a good ride. The following tips might also be of help:

- Choose your route. Consider the ability/ experience of each rider in your group. Check the weather forecast. How much time do you have available?
- Study the route description carefully before setting off. Cross-reference this to the relevant map so that you've got a good sense of general orientation in case you need an escape route.
- Tell somebody where you're going and when you'll be back.
- Set out well equipped and properly clothed, carry sufficient food and water and pack your tools, a tube, a pump and any necessary spare parts.
- **Get out there and get dirty!**

Hold on... read this

Safety warnings

Many routes are challenging and include tough climbs and steep descents, which can potentially be very dangerous. Too much exuberance on a slippery descent in the middle of nowhere could leave you in trouble, especially if you're alone. Consider your limitations and relative fragility before attempting some of the harder routes in the book, which are aimed at the fit and technically accomplished mountain biker.

Some of these routes venture into remote and difficult terrain, where you don't really want to run into problems. If you are planning to tackle these you'll need a bit of what's best described as moorland 'savvy' – particularly on shorter, winter days.

Be self-sufficient. Carry plenty of food and water. Take your spares, a tube and a pump. Consider a first-aid kit. Even if it's warm at the start, it could be chilly higher up or later in the day, so take a wind/ waterproof. Think about what could happen in the case of an enforced stop. Pack a good light if there's a risk of finishing in the dark.

The ability to read a map, navigate in poor visibility and understand weather warnings should also be treated as essential.

If you're riding solo, think about the potential seriousness of an accident – you could be without assistance for a considerable length of time. Tell someone where you are going and when to expect you back. Take a mobile phone if you have one, but don't rely on getting a signal. (And please don't call mountain rescue out just because you've grazed your knee.)

Riding in a group is safer and usually more fun, but don't leave the slower members of your party too far behind. Allow extra time for a group ride, as you'll inevitably be dealing with punctures or mechanicals. You may need an extra top if you end up standing around for a while. Finally, don't crash into your mates.

As the area is a popular destination, please ride within your ability and give way to other users. Yes, bells are annoying and we don't like them either, but they do work. If you can't bring yourself to bolt one on, a polite "excuse me" works fine.

On hot, sunny days, make sure you slap on the Factor 30+ and always wear a helmet!

Mountain Rescue

In the event of an accident requiring mountain rescue assistance:
Dial 999 and ask for POLICE – MOUNTAIN RESCUE.

A basic knowledge of first aid, a map to provide mountain rescue with your location and warm clothing will all be of great help in an emergency.

Rights of way

To the best of our knowledge, all of the routes in this guide are totally legal and mountain bikers have what is termed 'Right of Way'. (This doesn't mean that you actually have the right of way – you don't – just that you are allowed to be there in the first place.)

Here are some points about why it's a good idea to stick to legal trails:

1. We have not always had the access to the countryside that we enjoy today. Some pioneering folk worked very hard to gain it and it would be a shame to jeopardise this hard-won freedom through careless or ill-informed actions. It could also make you pretty unpopular with other riders.

2. Technically speaking, you're committing trespass if you ride on a footpath – no matter how wide – and you could be prosecuted by the landowner for any damage caused. Also, most sensible people would rather avoid the embarrassment involved in this kind of confrontation.

3. Riding on footpaths upsets walkers, who have every right to enjoy their day.

4. Sticking to rights of way helps preserve fragile moorland habitats, whereas bashing through overgrown greenery will play havoc with your shifting.

Rights of way include

Footpaths:
Usually the most tempting, narrowest and swoopiest trails around, but off-limits to mountain bikers. Please don't ride them – you've no right to be there, you will upset and possibly endanger other users, and won't do the sport's reputation any good at all.

Bridleways
Trails for horses! And bikes! Mountain bikers have the right to share bridleways with walkers and horses – but take care, horses spook easily.

Byways Open to All Traffic
Otherwise known as BOATs, these allow all traffic access, including vehicles – although, surprisingly, we've yet to see a boat on a BOAT. This means that you may well be sharing the trail with motorcyclists and 4WD enthusiasts – often to be seen enjoying the peace, quiet and fresh air of the countryside.

Forest Tracks and Paths

Officially, you need permission to ride on Forestry Commission land. However, this has often been granted, and the Forestry Commission generally regards cycling favourably. A note of caution: beware of forestry operations – a fully loaded logging truck could easily scuff your paintwork and dent *you*!

Green Lanes

A non-legal term for an unsurfaced country road. There is some debate as to who's allowed to use them, but mountain bikers have nothing to worry about at present.

White Roads

On maps, most roads are coloured to indicate their status. White roads aren't and so have no recorded status. They often appear to be farm tracks or private roads when they are actually public highways. There are an estimated 7000km of 'lost' white roads around the UK, many are great, totally legal trails. (You need to check the definitive map at your local highway authority to be absolutely sure – if in doubt stick to a bridleway.) **If you're not familiar with the symbols denoting bridleways, footpaths and so on, check the information section on your map.**

Signs

Not all tracks are signed. What this means is that it's not necessarily obvious whether that great-looking trail you want to follow is an illegal footpath or a legal bridleway. That's why it's a good idea to carry a map with you on every ride.

Many paths do carry signs with coloured arrows which depict their status. These are:

Yellow: Footpaths (you know the rules)
Blue: Bridleways (go for it! Watching out for walkers and horses, mind...)
Red: Byways (that can be used by everyone)

Some forestry areas also have waymarked cycle routes. These colouring systems usually indicate the difficulty of the route – look out for explanatory notices at the trailhead.

Rules of the (off) road

Only hooligans enjoy the stress of conflict. The mountain biking community deserves a big pat on the back for keeping it chill on the hill – let's keep it that way:

1. Always ride on legal trails.
2. Ride considerately – give way to horses and pedestrians.
3. Don't spook animals – avoid natural habitats, flocks of sheep and crops.

4. Ride in control – you don't know who's around the next corner.
5. Leave gates as you find them – if you're unsure, shut them.
6. Keep the noise down and don't swear loudly when you fall off in front of walkers.
7. Leave no trace – take home everything you took out.
8. Keep water sources clean – don't take toilet stops near streams.
9. Be self-sufficient – you and your bike.
10. Enjoy the countryside and respect its life and work.

Bike setup

Check everything's working – you won't be going uphill fast if your gears seize, but you'll go a little faster than planned if your brakes don't work. It can also be annoying when parts fall off. Pump the tyres up, check nothing's about to wear through and make sure that everything that should be tight is tight. If you can't do this yourself, visit your local shop.

Frame and Forks

Personally, we wouldn't take a 40lb 9" travel monster on these routes and we wouldn't pick a fully rigid singlespeed. If you would, go for it!

Seriously now, a full suspension bike will add comfort and control. A lightweight race number will make hills easier and something with a bit of travel will help on technical descents. Ideally, we'd pick the best compromise between all three.

What tyres for... ?

Most of the rides in this book call for all-round tyres. However, in winter you might consider a mud tyre essential, whilst in the dry, few can deny that a fast tyre is more fun. A few of the routes tackle fast and rocky terrain, so something with a bit of size might help as far as comfort and puncture prevention go.

Essential kit

Helmet

"The best helmet is the one that you're wearing". Just make sure that it fits, that you're wearing it correctly and that it won't move around in a crash.

Clothing

The tried and tested layering system utilising wicking fabrics (not cotton) works really well, especially in winter. As mountain biking is a very active sport, it's worth setting off just a little on the cool side – you'll soon warm up. Padded shorts are definitely more comfortable, but the amount of lycra on show is your choice.

Don't, however, make the mistake of leaving those essential warm layers behind, as you'll need them on the descents and during snack breaks.

Gloves
Gloves help prevent blisters and numb hands and keep your fingers warm in the winter. They also provide a surprising amount of protection when you come off.

Footwear
Flat pedals/ SPDs – your call. They aren't going to grip on wet limestone, so don't worry about that, but make sure they have sufficient tread for everywhere else. Consider over-shoes if it's chilly.

Other Essentials
Take any necessary spares, tools, a tube and a pump, spare clothes, first aid kit, food and water. Stop short of the kitchen sink, though, as you still want to be able to ride your bike.

You'll need something to carry it all in. We'd suggest a hydration pack, as they keep the weight off the bike, allow you to carry more and let you drink on the move more easily.

Maps

Harvey Maps:
- Yorkshire Dales South
- Yorkshire Dales East
- Yorkshire Dales West

Ordnance Survey:
- OL2 Yorkshire Dales: Southern and Western Areas
- OL30 Yorkshire Dales: Northern and Central Areas
- OL41 Forest of Bowland and Ribblesdale
- Explorer 298 Nidderdale
- Explorer 302 Northallerton and Thirsk

Night riding
Night riding opens up a whole new world of fun. Now it's possible to enjoy an after-work ride in the depths of winter in your favourite off-road playground. Night riding is brilliant fun, but it's a completely different ball game and (hardly surprisingly) there are a few risks to be aware of. To help stay out of trouble, here are a few tips:

Lights and Batteries
Invest carefully in a lighting system. We've been using the excellent Lumicycle range. Consider battery life, weight, number of bulbs and power. Ensure that your battery is fully

PHOTO COURTESY OF LUMICYCLE

charged before you ride (sounds like common sense, but we've done it!). Carry a secondary light source such as a head torch for emergencies (it's surprising what you can ride with a commuter light if you have to, although it isn't much fun). Ensure that you pack a rear light for road sections and keep it clear of mud.

Route Planning and Safety

Choose your ride on the basis of battery life. (Time it yourself, don't necessarily rely on the manufacturer's information.) Allow extra time – you will be slower in the dark. Stay on ground that you are familiar with at first (night-time navigation in unfamiliar territory demands military expertise) and not too far from home. Always ride with a friend. Watch out for the werewolves. Make sure that someone knows where you're going and when to expect you back.

Ride within your limits – trees loom up very quickly in the dark!

Thanks to:

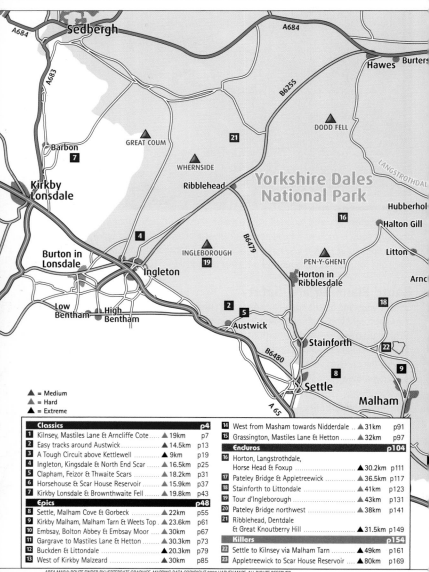

Yorkshire Dales
Mountain**Biking**
Area Map & Route Finder

SECTION 1

Classics

A quick blast after work, a night loop you can finish before your lights run dry, or a ride to squeeze in when you're short of time. That's a classic. Relatively low on distance and never taking you too far from the start, these are still good, solid rides.

Short, but not necessarily easy.

Classics
sponsored by **bike**magic.com

www.bikemagic.com

CLASSICS

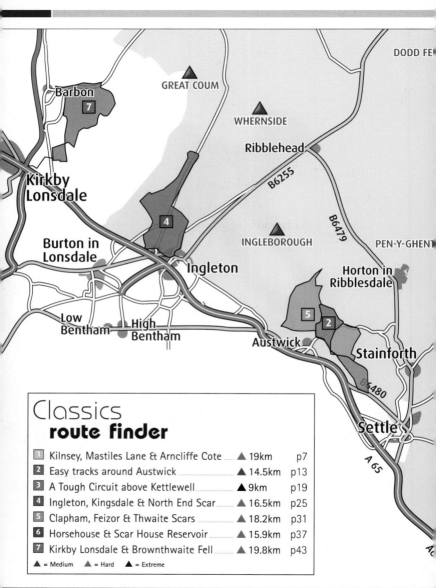

DODD FE

GREAT COUM

WHERNSIDE

Ribblehead

B6255

Barbon

7

Kirkby
Lonsdale

4

Burton in
Lonsdale

INGLEBOROUGH

B6479

PEN-Y-GHENT

Ingleton

Horton in
Ribblesdale

Low
Bentham — High
Bentham

5 **2**

Austwick

Stainforth

B6480

Settle

Classics
route finder

▲ = Medium   ▲ = Hard   ▲ = Extreme

A 65

Yorkshire Dales National Park

LANGSTROTHDALE

B6160

Horsehouse

Cray
BUCKDEN PIKE

Hubberholme

Buckden

WHARFEDALE

6

Halton Gill

Starbotton

Litton

B6160

3

GREAT WHERNSIDE

Arncliffe

LITTONDALE

Kettlewell

NIDDERDALE

Hawkswick

1 Kilnsey

Conistone

Threshfield

Grassington

B6

Linton

Hebden

WHARFEDALE

Malham

Thorpe

Skyreholme

Cracoe

Appletreewick

Hetton

Hellifield

A65

Classics Route Finder

Kilnsey, Mastiles Lane & Arncliffe Cote

19km

Introduction

This is in many ways the perfect half-day trip, with all of the tracks rideable by reasonably fit, skilled mountain bikers except in the wettest/softest/muddiest conditions. The longest and toughest climb is at the start of the ride, rewarded by a long undulating section along the historic drovers' road known as Mastiles Lane; the second climb sets you up for a dream descent on easy grassy tracks with superb views down into the wooded valley of Littondale, dropping 300m to Arncliffe Cote and an easy tarmac finish beneath the sphinx-like rock outcrop of Kilnsey Crag back to a good pub. It is also one of those rides that is just as good in reverse.

The Ride

Climb west from the pub in Kilnsey, at first steeply on tarmac then more steadily off-road along a fine stone track over Kilnsey Moor. After the first major summit there are two more minor highpoints along this undulating track, the surface of which varies from stone to grass and very occasionally rough and cut up by off-road vehicles. Just before rejoining tarmac at Street Gate turn sharply uphill (northeast) on the second leg of the route, climbing on a grassy track up to the highest point of the ride (510m), setting you up for a grand, nay champion(!) descent above the steep valley of Cote Gill and down to Arncliffe Cote for a short tarmac cruise back to Kilnsey.

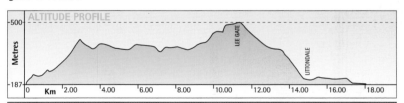

ALTITUDE PROFILE

Metres: -500- / -187-

Km | 2.00 | 4.00 | 6.00 | 8.00 | 10.00 | 12.00 | 14.00 | 16.00 | 18.00

LEE GATE

LITTONDALE

KILNSEY, MASTILES LANE & ARNCLIFFE COTE   GRADE:

DISTANCE: 19KM   **TOTAL ASCENT:** 525M

START/FINISH: KILNSEY, ON THE B6160 NORTH OF GRASSINGTON   **GRID REFERENCE: 1.** 973 688 / **2.** 973 677

PARKING: NONE IN THE CENTRE OF KILNSEY ITSELF. TWO OPTIONS:

1. THE LARGE LAYBY NEAR THE B6160 JUNCTION WITH THE ARNCLIFFE ROAD NORTH OF KILNSEY

2. ON THE LANE CLIMBING WEST FROM THE TENNANT ARMS IN KILNSEY SIGNPOSTED *UNSUITABLE FOR MOTORS.* FOLLOW FOR APPROX 600M TO A LARGE LAYBY BEYOND A GATE/CATTLEGRID AT GR 973 677

PUBLIC HOUSE: TENNANT ARMS, KILNSEY Tel: 01756 752301   **CAFÉ:** BRING SANDWICHES

Kilnsey, Mastiles Lane & Arncliffe Cote

Directions – Kilnsey, Mastiles Lane & Arncliffe Cote

❺ With your back to the Tennant Arms in Kilnsey turn **R** then **R** again on the lane signposted *Unsuitable for motors*. Climb steeply for 650m. As the tarmac road continues up to the right bear **L** onto a broad gravel track signposted *Route to Malham, no cars or motorbikes*. After 500m at a fork of broad stone tracks bear **L** signposted *Route to Malham Tarn*.

2 Climb steadily for 2.5km to the first summit then follow the undulating track for a further 5km over a variety of surfaces. At the gate just **before** rejoining tarmac by a *Kilnsey 5 miles* signpost pointing back the way you have come, **do not** go through the gate but turn **R** uphill (northeast) on a grassy track (GR 905 656).

3 After 800m and shortly after passing through a gate with a *No cars* sign, then a ford and a wet section, the track swings sharp **R** uphill (GR 909 665).

4 Climb to the highpoint then, following signs for *Arncliffe Cote*, descend on a superb, broad, well-drained grass track. All forks rejoin as you aim towards the static caravans down in the valley at Arncliffe Cote.

5 Join tarmac by the farm then shortly at the road turn **R** for 3km.

6 At the T-junction with the B6160 turn **R** signposted *Grassington, Skipton* to return to the start.

◀◉⊃ **Making a day of it**

Three other rides use sections of Mastiles Lane: those starting from *Kirkby Malham – see page 61*, *Grassington – see page 97* and *Gargrave – see page 73*. Just 2km northwest of Arncliffe Cote you can link to the *Buckden–Littondale ride – see page 79*.

NARROW LANES FROM WHARFE

Easy tracks around **Austwick**

14.5km

Introduction

One of the easiest rides in the book, this nevertheless gives a good taste of all that is typical and best about off-road riding in the Yorkshire Dales. A good pub in an attractive village at the start, walled lanes and tracks with field barns everywhere, fords and woodland, one or two bits just hard enough to test to see if you can ride them without a dab and a great rollercoaster grassy descent down to Feizor. One to take reluctant riders on to convince them!

The Ride

Leave Austwick to the north on a walled dead-end lane climbing 100m as you spin the pedals to warm up. Turning off this track you soon have the option of a ford or a stone clapper bridge. The track narrows and there are one or two rocks to give the forks a workout. Walled tracks take you through the settlement of Wharfe and to the start of the second climb (120m) passing to the south of Feizor Wood with one or two tricky rock steps. A climb on tarmac then a steep grassy push takes you to the highpoint of the ride. This smooth grassy track turns into a rollercoaster descent with lots of jump possibilities. The outward route is briefly rejoined before your return to the Game Cock in Austwick. Doesn't get much easier than that, does it?

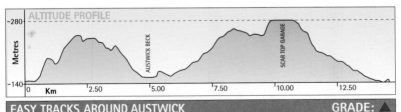

ALTITUDE PROFILE

AUSTWICK BECK

SCAR TOP GARAGE

Metres

-280

-140

0   Km   2.50   5.00   7.50   10.00   12.50

EASY TRACKS AROUND AUSTWICK

GRADE: ▲

DISTANCE: 14.5KM

START/FINISH: AUSTWICK, NORTHWEST OF SETTLE

PARKING: ON STREET PARKING NEAR GAME COCK PUB

PUBLIC HOUSE: GAME COCK Tel: 015242 51226, AUSTWICK OR OFF THE ROUTE IN SETTLE

TOTAL ASCENT: 325M

GRID REFERENCE: 768 685

CAFÉ: BRING SANDWICHES

Easy tracks around Austwick

Directions – Easy tracks
around Austwick

➲ With your back to the Game Cock Inn in Austwick turn **L** (towards Helwith Bridge). Immediately after passing the primary school turn **L** onto Townhead Lane (no through road).

2 Climb steadily on tarmac past the last of the houses and to the end of the tarmac (shortly after Sowerthwaite Farm). About 500m after the end of tarmac, by a *No vehicles ½ mile ahead* signpost turn **R** onto a wide track signposted *Bridleway to Wharfe*.

3 Cross the ford or the stone clapper bridge. After a long gentle descent, at the T-junction by a cluster of houses turn **L** then follow the main track round to the **R**. At the T-junction with the road by a barn bear **R** then shortly take the first wide stone track to the **L** signposted *Woodend Farm, Wood Lane Bridleway*.

4 Follow the walled track to the **R** by the farm then round a sharp **LH** bend. Ignore a wide track off to the left just before a telegraph pole. At an offset X-roads of tracks turn sharp **L** uphill on a wide stone track.

5 Go past a house on the left. The track narrows. At a fork of tracks with a barn to the right bear **R** close to the barn. Can you ride it all without a dab? At the junction with the road go **SA** signposted *Settle*.

6 At the T-junction with the B6480 by a *Give Way* sign turn **L**. Shortly after the start of the descent, opposite Scar Top Garage turn **L** through a narrow wooden gate signposted *Bridleway to Feizor*.

7 Short steep grassy climb between rocky outcrops. As the gradient eases turn **L** through a narrow wooden gate in the wall to your left by a *Footpath to Giggleswick* signpost (pointing right). Keep following the broad smooth grassy track through a series of gates, passing a wooden *Buck Haw Brow/Stackhouse* signpost.

◄⊙◯ Making a day of it

The *Clapham & Feizor* ride – *see page 31* – overlaps with this one. Other nearby rides start from Settle, *see pages 55 & 161* , Stainforth, *see page 123*, and Horton in Ribblesdale, *see page 111*.

8 Great rolling grassy descent with a chance for jumps. At the T-junction with the road by a cluster of buildings in Feizor turn **L*** then **R** onto a concrete road alongside a new barn signposted *Bridleway to Austwick*.

* **OR** for a link to the *Clapham & Feizor Ride* turn **R** here (see page 31)

9 The concrete turns to track and narrows. At a T-junction of tracks with a barn ahead bear **R** to rejoin the outward route. Go past a house on the right then at the next track junction follow the main track round to the **L**. At the T-junction with tarmac turn **R** then shortly **R** again to return to the start.

TOM FENTON SLOGGING AWAY

A **Tough Circuit** above **Kettlewell** 9km

Introduction

This small but perfectly formed loop will have your lungs and legs screaming on the climb and whooping with delight on the downhill. It would take a pretty good rider to be able to cycle the first 1.5km of this route without a dab. The total climb for the whole ride is only 310m, small fry compared to some of the longer rides but the first 150m of climbing occurs in the first 1.5km, a very steep road climb followed by a very steep off-road climb on a broad stone track with enough loose stone to make choosing the best line a real test. The descent is one to do over and over, as fast as your handling skills and bottle will let you!

The Ride

Make your way through the attractive village of Kettlewell and don't stuff yourself full of cakes in the many cafes *just* yet. You will need to be in top condition to attack first the very steep tarmac lane climbing out of Kettlewell towards Coverdale then the very steep broad track climbing straight up the ridge towards Top Mere. A gate signals an easing in the gradient and the climb now becomes possible for mere mortals, not superheroes. There is very little contouring around the hillside before the descent starts and it has a bit of everything, bends and berms and grassy strips, solid rock and loose rock. Yippee! Let's do that again.

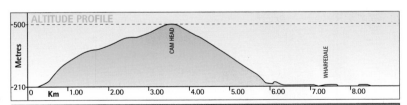

A TOUGH CIRCUIT ABOVE KETTLEWELL   GRADE: ▲

DISTANCE: 9KM

START/FINISH: KETTLEWELL

TOTAL ASCENT: 340M

GRID REFERENCE: 968 722

PARKING: THE CAR PARK OPERATED BY THE GARAGE IS CHEAPER THAN THE 'OFFICIAL' PAY & DISPLAY

PUBLIC HOUSE: LOTS OF CHOICE IN KETTLEWELL

        FOX & HOUNDS, STARBOTTON Tel: 01756 760269

CAFÉ: LOTS OF CHOICE IN KETTLEWELL

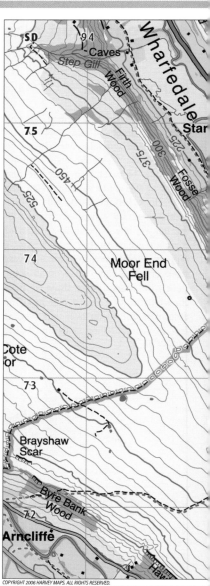

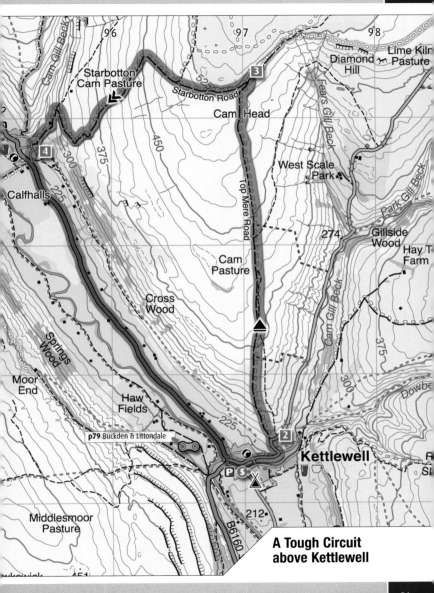

A Tough Circuit
above Kettlewell

Directions – A Tough Circuit
above Kettlewell

➊ With your back to the Blue Bell Inn in the centre of Kettlewell turn **L** signposted *Coverdale*. At the X-roads by Kettlewell Village Store go **SA** signposted *Leyburn*.

2 Very steep climb on tarmac. Go round a sharp left-hand bend then on a sharp right-hand bend bear **L** signposted *Bridleway to Starbotton*. Very steep climb on broad stone track.

3 The gradient eases after 800m after going through a gate. At the T-junction after 2km by a 3-way signpost turn **L** signposted *Starbotton* (GR 970 753).

4 Absolute top grade descent. At the junction with the B6160 in Starbotton at the bottom turn **L** to return to Kettlewell.

◄☉☉ **Making a day of it**

You may want to do this loop more than once, or try it in reverse or even use the road up to Coverdale to gain height then use the bridleway running west from near the cattlegrid at the summit (GR 987 758) to access the top of Cam Head for a choice of descents. For a longer ride this could be easily zipped together with the *Buckden–Littondale* ride – *see page 79*. Another near-by ride, the one starting from *Kilnsey – see page 7* – is best accessed via the back lane down to Coniston as the B6160 is a busy road.

YORKSHIRE IS FAMOUS FOR ITS DRYSTONE WALLS

Ingleton, Kingsdale & North End Scar

16.5km

Introduction

Ingleton – Land of Caves and Waterfalls and the popular Ingleton Waterfall Walk – so go easy near the town on a sunny bank holiday. This is quintessential Dales scenery: limestone and drystone walls, sheep and rough pastures, narrow lanes and enclosed tracks – and this route encompasses them all. Although never overly technical, the riding is still hard and you will struggle on the unsigned track climbing out of Kingsdale. It soon eases, with views ahead as far as Morecambe Bay, At one point, you can hear rushing water, but it's all happening underground... The ride continues on a loose descent and a lane network to the Marton Arms, one of the best pubs around with a mighty array of real ales. Wobble back to Ingleton.

The Ride

Climb steeply out of Ingleton on tarmac up to Scar End and the start of the dirt (and rock). Leave the hordes of waterfall-walkers (you'll see!) behind as you descend to cross Kingsdale Beck via the ford or the bridge and join the lane along the bottom of Kingsdale – enclosed by some of the finest sections of drystone wall in the National Park. You get a lot of time to look at drystone walls from the saddle of a bike! The turn off the lane is easy to miss and the track is initially very hard work, a steep uphill slog to gain the grassy track above (initially rather indistinct). Cruise along this, admiring the views, to a loose and rocky descent dropping down to some quiet lanes which lead back to Ingleton.

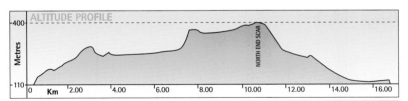

ALTITUDE PROFILE

NORTH END SCAR

Metres

-400

-110

| 0 | Km | 2.00 | 4.00 | 6.00 | 8.00 | 10.00 | 12.00 | 14.00 | 16.00 |

INGLETON, KINGSDALE & NORTH END SCAR   GRADE:

DISTANCE: 16.5KM

START/FINISH: THE MAIN CHURCH IN THE CENTRE OF INGLETON

PARKING: SEVERAL PAY & DISPLAY CAR PARKS IN INGLETON

TOTAL ASCENT: 423M

GRID REFERENCE: 695 733

CAFÉ: LOTS OF CHOICE IN INGLETON

PUBLIC HOUSE: LOTS OF CHOICE IN INGLETON, MARTON ARMS HOTEL, THORNTON Tel: 015 242 42358

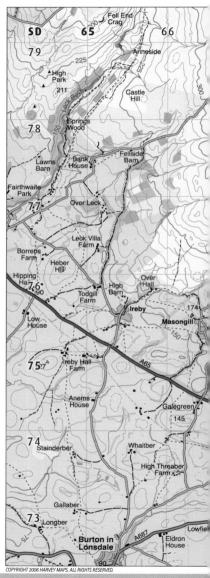

Ingleton, Kingsdale & North End Scar

Directions – Ingleton, Kingsdale & North End Scar

5 From the main church in Ingleton descend towards the river (the first 50m is the wrong way on a one way road, so walk) then turn **R** just before the bridge onto Mill Lane.

2 Climb steeply for 1.6km then immediately after a sharp right-hand bend turn **L** through a gate (GR 699 745) onto an unfenced lane towards Twisleton Hall. Continue climbing, pass between buildings and follow the road round to the **L**. The tarmac turns to track.

3 Climb then descend to cross the footbridge over Kingsdale Beck or go through the ford. At the T-junction with the road turn **R** and follow for 3.5km.

4 **Easy to miss:** at a clump of about 50 trees, and just before a short climb, turn **L** through a wooden field gate (GR 707 790 – no sign) and bear **L** on a steeply rising faint grass track running parallel with the stone wall to the right.

5 It looks very unpromising but continue in the same direction uphill after the end of the trees on the right, parallel with the wall, to go through the gate in the top right-hand corner of the field. Turn **L** on a rough track. Initially a little vague, the condition of the track improves in the next field.

6 Flat or gentle climb for 3km then a fine descent for 1km. Opposite a stone barn (a water treatment plant) on the right (GR 676 763), turn **L** onto a broad stone track.

7 At the T-junction with the road at the end of the track turn **R**. After 750m, on a sharp right-hand bend take the first lane to the **L** signposted *No through road, unsuitable for motors*. At the T-junction after 1km turn **L**.

8 Go past the Marton Arms Hotel then at the next T-junction (GR 687 734) bear **L** signposted *Clapham, Settle*. Descend into Ingleton, cross the bridge over the river and climb back up to the start.

◄◎ **Making a day of it**
Another ride starts from *Ingleton*, a long anti-clockwise circuit of *Ingleborough – see page 131.*

MYSTERIOUS TUNNEL NEAR CLAPHAM

Clapham, Feizor & Thwaite Scars   18.2km

Introduction

In many ways this is the perfect short Dales ride with two attractive villages and two small hamlets linked by a series of tracks that range from broad stone to singletrack and from quiet lanes to a high grassy plateau in amongst a sea of limestone pavement. It is a ride starting with a tough climb and finishing with a fine descent, with the added spice of long dark tunnels to navigate. Passing through a scenery of pasture grazed by sheep and cattle, the ride explores a landscape dotted with field barns, old stone farmhouses, clumps of broadleaf woodland and a riot of wildflowers in the spring.

The Ride

Head for the church in Clapham and onto a broad stone track that soon enters two tunnels – somewhat disorientating in the sudden darkness – and make your way uphill on cobbles. Climb out into quintessential Dales scenery with tall stone walls either side of the track and rocky outcrops up to the left. Weave your way along the spider's web of tracks and lanes, including the alternative challenges of a ford or a narrow stone clapper bridge. Climb up past Feizor Wood, descend to Wharfe then climb again onto the high grassy plateau of Long Scar. Waymarks are scarce on the ground but if you keep climbing you'll reach the main track from Selside to Clapham – turn sharp left and enjoy a long grass and then stone descent to rejoin the outward route for a second chance at the tunnels, this time downhill.

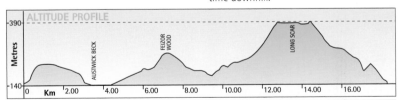

ALTITUDE PROFILE

Metres: -390 ... -140

Km: 0   2.00   4.00   6.00   8.00   10.00   12.00   14.00   16.00

AUSTWICK BECK   FEIZOR WOOD   LONG SCAR

CLAPHAM, FEIZOR AND THWAITE SCARS   GRADE:

DISTANCE: 18.2KM

START/FINISH: CLAPHAM, NORTHWEST OF SETTLE

PARKING: PAY & DISPLAY IN THE CENTRE OF CLAPHAM

CAFÉ: CAFÉ ANNE Tel: 01524 251716,
BROOKHOUSE CAFÉ Tel: 015 242 51580, BOTH IN CLAPHAM

TOTAL ASCENT: 472M

GRID REFERENCE: 745 693

PUBLIC HOUSE: NEW INN, CLAPHAM Tel: 015 242 51203

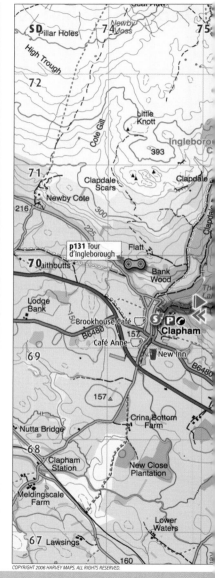

p131 Tour d'Ingleborough

Clapham, Feizor and Thwaite Scars

Directions – Clapham, Feizor and Thwaite Scars

⊘ With your back to the New Inn in Clapham turn **R** along Church Avenue, signposted *National Park Centre*, keeping Clapham Beck to your left. At the church turn **R** onto a broad stone track that soon swings **L**, signposted *Bridleway to Austwick*. Go through two tunnels. Climb steeply for 800m to the summit. **Ignore** a wide stone track to the left signposted *Bridleway to Selside* (this is the return route).

2 After 1.6km, at a X-roads with a minor lane go **SA** onto the broad stone track opposite. Gentle descent. At the road turn **R** then after 400m, and immediately after a stone barn on the left, turn **L** onto a broad stone track signposted *Bridleway to Feizor*.

3 Follow this narrower stone track to a ford or clapper bridge over the stream. The next section is stone-based but narrow and may be overgrown. At the junction of tracks (GR 777 684) turn **R** uphill on a broader farm track, soon passing a telegraph pole on your left. The track narrows again after a house (Wood House) on the left with a short loose rock section. The next stretch may be overgrown in summer.

4 At a fork of tracks by a stone barn (Meldings Barn) bear **L** towards a steep hill. The track broadens and turns to concrete at the next barn (Cat Hole Barn). At the T-junction with the road by the farm in Feizor turn **L**.

5 The tarmac turns to track after 1km. Ignore a track with a gate to the left at the top of the climb. About 500m after the summit, ignore the next stone track into a farm (Higher Bark House) on the left. Follow the main stone track through the next farm (Lower Bark House) then at the road turn **L**.

6 After 800m, on a sharp left-hand bend, bear **R** onto a broad stone track signposted *Private road, public footpath and bridleway only*. At the top of the climb, shortly after a left-hand bend and opposite an old stone barn turn **R** uphill signposted *Bridleway*. Keep following this track round to the **R**, on grass and occasionally through what feels like people's gardens to join a better track which narrows then widens again.

7 At the T-junction with boulders and cliffs ahead (GR 772 706) turn **R** signposted *No cars after ½ mile*. After 800m at a fork by a clump of trees bear **L** onto a grassy bridleway (not the private track to the right to Crummack). Shortly turn **L** steeply uphill at a wooden *Bridleway* signpost then after 200m at a faint fork of grassy tracks bear **R** on the upper track.

8 Route finding is tricky for the next 1.2km, as there are many more tracks on the ground than are shown on the map and no waymarks until you reach the top. Keep bearing **R** to turn north, above the limestone pavement. Continue in the same direction on the grass or grass & stone track. At a stone and cement cairn with a tumbledown wall up ahead, turn sharp **L** back on yourself onto a grass and stone track (GR 773 724).

9 Follow the cairns southwest towards a second stone and cement cairn. Lots of tracks, no signs: take care in mist/fog/heavy rain. You are aiming to drop down to the right (to the west, in other words) on a grass/grass & stone track, through two gates to join a well-defined stone track (starting at GR 758 716) with huge views ahead.

10 After the first loose section, there is a rough, but mainly firm, stone descent over the next 2.5km. At the T-junction of stone tracks turn **R** to rejoin the outward route. Go back down through the tunnels, past the church to return to Clapham.

◄☎ Making a day of it

This ride could be bolted on to the *Tour d'Ingleborough – see page 131 –* to make it even longer. Start with this ride then once up onto Long Scar (the end of **8**, GR 773 724), turn **right** and join the other ride towards Selside then Horton. It would also be easy to link to the *Stainforth* ride east of Helwith Bridge – *see page 123*. Other nearby rides start from *Horton – see page 111 – Settle – see pages 55 & 161 –* and *Ingleton – see page 25*.

SCAR HOUSE RESERVOIR

Horsehouse & Scar House Reservoir 15.9km

Introduction

There are disappointingly few decent rideable tracks leading east or west from the scenic road through Coverdale – they either start with promise and peter out or start badly and continue that way, so make the most of this lollipop-shaped ride south from the hamlet of Horsehouse over Arkleside Moor down to Scar House Reservoir. The challenge up and over the moor is one to store away in your memory as you complete an easy circuit of the spectacularly set reservoir, knowing that what was a tough climb on the outward leg becomes a blistering downhill on the return.

The Ride

Roll down the hill from the Thwaite Inn in Horsehouse, cross the River Cover at Arkleside Bridge and prepare for the long climb over Arkleside Moor, at first steeply then more gently to a highpoint of 550 metres with views soon opening up down to both Scar House and Angram Reservoirs. The descent is steeper than the climb, rougher, looser and at times washed out. One to test your skills. The circuit of Scar House Reservoir is on a permissive bridleway and is straightforward – the south side runs along a tarmac lane. At the eastern end of the reservoir you have the option of extending the ride further east on the Nidderdale Way, running high above the valley. The return climb may prove unrideable in parts but sets you up for a dream descent back to Horsehouse.

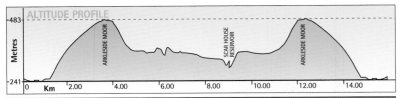

ALTITUDE PROFILE

ARKLESIDE MOOR / SCAR HOUSE RESERVOIR / ARKLESIDE MOOR

Metres — 483 / 241

Km 2.00 4.00 6.00 8.00 10.00 12.00 14.00

HORSEHOUSE & SCAR HOUSE RESERVOIR GRADE: △

DISTANCE: 15.9KM

TOTAL ASCENT: 550M

START/FINISH: HORSEHOUSE, IN COVERDALE TO THE NORTHEAST OF KETTLEWELL

GRID REFERENCE: 815 048

PARKING: ON THE ROADSIDE WHERE IT WIDENS AT THE NORTH END OF THE VILLAGE

PUBLIC HOUSE: THWAITE INN, HORSEHOUSE Tel: 01969 640206

CAFÉ: BRING SANDWICHES

Horsehouse & Scar House Reservoir

Directions – Horsehouse &
Scar House Reservoir

➎ With your back to the Thwaite Inn in Horsehouse turn **L**. After 600m take the first road **L** signposted *Arkleside only, unsuitable for motors*. At a fork of tracks soon after the tarmac ends, turn **L** uphill through a gate.

2 Very steep then easier gradient on the 2.5km climb (240m of ascent) to the highpoint.

3 Mixed quality descent. At the junction of tracks at the bottom go **SA** over the stream signposted *Footpath* (it is in fact a permissive bridleway). Go through a gate then with *Circular Walk* signposted ahead **and** to the right, turn **R** on a track running parallel with the reservoir to your left.

4 Go through several more gates. At the Angram Reservoir dam turn **L** then at the end of the dam turn **L** again. Easy tarmac section.

5 After 2.2km turn **L** to cross the Scar House Reservoir dam. At the end of the dam bear **L** uphill on a broad 'cobbled' track (in other words, not sharp left alongside the water). Shortly turn first **L** gently downhill on grass and stone track.

6 At the T-junction at the end of the 'loop' (GR 047 773) turn **R** uphill to rejoin the outward route. Follow the broad stone track up and over the hill. At the T-junction with the road turn **R** to return to Horsehouse.

◀◖◖◗ Making a day of it

This ride could easily be extended south all the way to *Pateley Bridge* – *see page 141* – by turning right at the eastern end of *Scar House Reservoir* instead of left. Other rides to the north are covered in this book's companion guide: **Yorkshire Dales Mountain Biking – The North Dales**.

DESCENDING BARBONDALE

Kirkby Lonsdale & Brownthwaite Fell

19.8km

Introduction

Lying just outside the National Park, this ride explores the fells running along the east side of the Lune Valley, with four off-road sections linked by stretches of quiet lane. The first and longest climb on a dead end lane takes you high above the River Lune with views to Morecambe Bay, the Lakeland fells and the Howgills. The descents from Brownthwaite Fell back to the Bullpot road then down to Barbondale are rough and challenging with a mixture of soft ground and loose rock set against dramatic fellside background. The remaining, gentler off-road sections are through mixed woodland and a long walled track with Andy Goldsworthy art installations: huge boulders 'captured' by drystone wall enclosures.

The Ride

The first 5km of the ride are uphill, first on tarmac and then on a broad stone track, passing just beneath Brownthwaite Fell. The descent is rough and loose, and can be muddy in winter. Tarmac leads to Bullpot Farm and the mixed surface track to Barbondale. Pick your way down with the great bulk of Castle Knott and Middleton Fell ahead until a quick jink and a bridge crossing brings you to a gentle wooded downhill alongside Barbon Beck. Hit the road, and climb to the final dirt section along Wandale Lane, a wide stone track with a steep climb at the start. This becomes a rolling descent back to Bindloss Farm, soon rejoining the outward route back to Devil's Bridge.

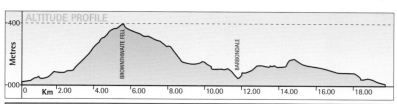

KIRKBY LONSDALE & BROWNTHWAITE FELL GRADE: ▲

DISTANCE: 19.8KM

TOTAL ASCENT: 454M

START/FINISH: DEVIL'S BRIDGE, KIRKBY LONSDALE, JUST NORTH OF THE JUNCTION OF THE A65 WITH THE A683

PARKING: ON THE EAST SIDE OF DEVIL'S BRIDGE

GRID REFERENCE: 616 783

PUBLIC HOUSE: LOTS OF CHOICE IN KIRKBY LONSDALE. BARBON INN, BARBON Tel: 015 242 76233

CAFÉ: LOTS OF CHOICE IN KIRKBY LONSDALE, TEA WAGON AT THE START

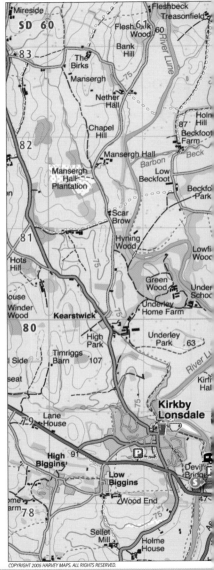

**Kirkby Lonsdale
& Brownthwaite Fell**

Directions – Kirkby Lonsdale
and Brownthwaite Fell

⑤ Go east from Devil's Bridge to cross the A683 (Sedbergh Road) opposite onto a one-way lane between stone walls. After 100m on a sharp right-hand bend bear **L** steeply uphill on a narrow lane. At the lane junction at the top of the steep climb bear **L** (in effect **SA**).

2 Go round one sharp left-hand bend. Shortly after the start of houses, on the next sharp left-hand bend take the lane on the **R**. Pass beneath the railway bridge. At the road junction at the top of the climb turn **L**. After 500m turn **R** at a X-roads of lanes onto a no through road signposted *Bullpot*.

3 Follow the lane **ignoring** a track to the left signposted *Unsuitable for motors* (this is the return route). Climb steeply on tarmac then turn **L** onto a broad grass and stone track between walls (GR 641 793) signposted *Footpath* (it actually has bridlepath status).

4 After 1km go though a gate and follow the track round to the **R**. Great views to the left and back down to Kirkby Lonsdale and the Lune Valley. The track passes to the **R** of the cairn up to your left and soon reaches the highpoint. Descend on track (at times muddy) to rejoin road and turn **L**.

5 At the T-junction of tracks at the end of the tarmac turn sharp **L**, soon descending on a mixed stone and earth track.

6 At the T-junction with the road turn **R** then shortly use the footbridge to cross Barbon Beck to your left and turn **L** onto a grass track.

7 After 1.4km **ignore** the first track to the right signposted *Private*. At a fork of tracks with a bridge to the left bear **R**. Emerge from the wood and bear **L** downhill on a tarmac drive.

8 Follow the drive to the church and turn **L** uphill on the lane. **Ignore** the first lane on the right. Cross the cattlegrid and take the next lane **R** sharply back on yourself.

9 After 1.5km, cross a second cattlegrid then turn **L** uphill onto a broad stone track signposted *Bridleway, Wandale Lane*. Short steep push then an easy 1.6km downhill. At the road go **SA*** signposted *Bridleway, Wandale Lane* for the full route.

* **OR** for a short cut, turn **R**, rejoining the outward route, for a direct lane route back to Devil's Bridge.

10 One overgrown section. **Easy to miss:** almost 1km after crossing the road turn **R** by a post with a blue arrow on a yellow background downhill on a wide grassy track between walls. The track jinks **R** then **L** towards Bindloss Farm, passing through gates.

11 Join a smooth gravel track by the farm. At the T-junction with the lane turn **R** then take the first lane **L** to rejoin the outward route. Go under the railway bridge, at the T-junction near houses turn **L**. Go round a sharp right-hand bend then on a sharp left-hand bend bear **R** downhill to return to the start.

⟜◯⊃ Making a day of it

Rides to the north in *Dentdale* are covered in this book's companion volume, ***Yorkshire Dales Mountain Biking – The North Dales***. Although the rides from Ingleton start only a few kilometres to the east of Kirkby Lonsdale, spending time on the very busy and dangerous A65, the only link between the two towns, is **not** recommended.

SECTION 2

Epics

*Getting longer now – these loops will take
a bit more time and effort. Not rides to be
scared of, but definitely rides to be respected.
Rather large hills and plenty of technical
ground to cover mean that firstly, you're
going to be out for a good few hours and
secondly, you're going to have a really
good time.*

Epics
sponsored by  SheCycles.com™

www.shecycles.com

APPROACHING MALHAM TARN

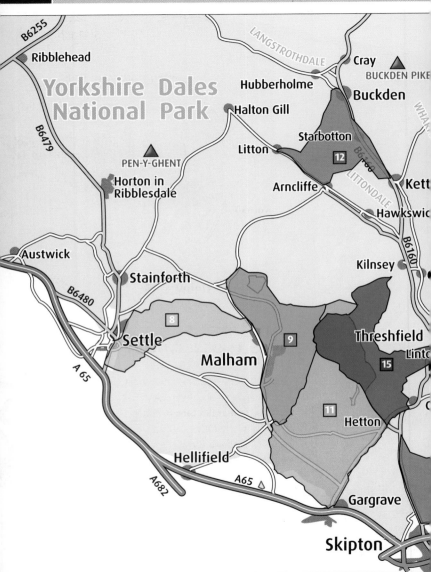

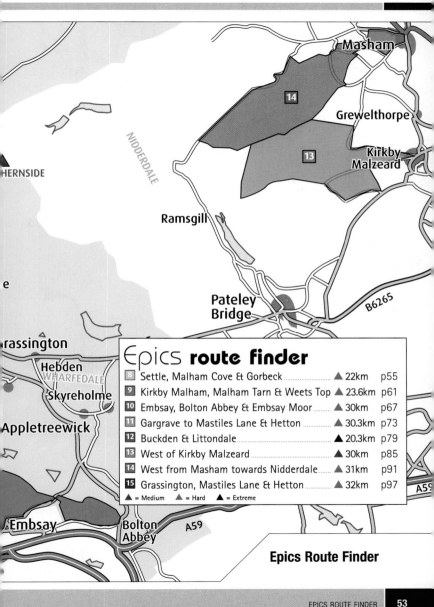

Epics Route Finder

A 'NARROW' DALES TRACK

Settle, Malham Cove & Gorbeck

22km

Introduction

Settle is one of the main settlements on the southern edge of the Park and has the added benefit of a bike shop by the station. Not hugely technical, but with some good fast sections and tough climbs, this route explores some stunning Dales scenery from broad tracks with sensational views. The return track over Gorbeck is an example of the Yorkshire Dales National Park Authority's hard work to restore trails over boggy ground. Although never technical, it is very fast, regardless of the weather.

The Ride

Head south out of Settle, picking up the start of the network of stone trails that lead up into the hills. Hit a tarmac lane and follow it towards Stockdale Farm before moving off-road and climbing over the rocky summit below Great Scar, via a couple of tricky rock gardens. The grassy descent heading towards Malham Cove is as wide and fast as you are willing! Joining the lane, turn left and climb back over Gorbeck on a newly constructed track across moorland. Straightforward and fast, this leads you rapidly to the Pennine Bridleway and a more interesting descent back into Settle.

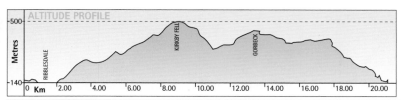

ALTITUDE PROFILE

500

Metres

RIBBLESDALE

KIRKBY FELL

GORBECK

140

0 Km 2.00 4.00 6.00 8.00 10.00 12.00 14.00 16.00 18.00 20.00

SETTLE, MALHAM COVE & GORBECK

GRADE:

DISTANCE: 22KM

START/FINISH: CENTRE OF SETTLE

PARKING: SEVERAL PAY & DISPLAY CAR PARKS IN SETTLE

CAFÉ: LOTS OF CHOICE IN SETTLE OR 1KM STEEPLY DOWN OFF THE ROUTE IN MALHAM

TOTAL ASCENT: 480M

GRID REFERENCE: 820 636

PUBLIC HOUSE: LOTS OF CHOICE IN SETTLE

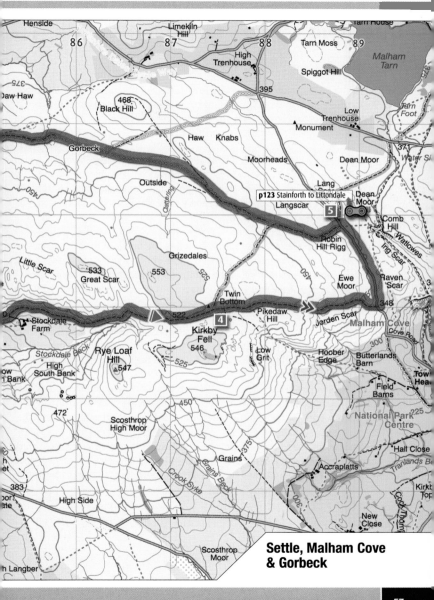

Settle, Malham Cove
& Gorbeck

Directions – Settle, Malham Cove & Gorbeck

⑤ Follow the B6480 south from the centre of Settle towards the railway station and Skipton. Go past the Falcon Manor Hotel then 800m after passing under the railway bridge turn **L** onto a broad stone track immediately before a low stone house and opposite a tall wooden *Settle* town sign (GR 813623).

2 Cross a bridge over the railway and climb steadily. Go through Lodge Farm, turn **L** then shortly at a fork bear **R** uphill between stone walls. Fine views back down to Settle. Keep climbing on 'cobble effect' trail. At a T-junction with a major stone track (GR 828624) turn **L** gently downhill then shortly turn first **R** sharply back on yourself signposted *Bridleway, Settle Loop*.

3 At the T-junction with the road turn **R** then take the first lane to the **L** signposted *Bridleway* and follow tarmac for 2.3km. At a fork of tracks at the end of the tarmac lane (with Stockdale Farm down to the right), bear **L** through a gate onto a narrower stone track alongside the wall. The stone track turns to grass then becomes rocky for the summit before turning back to grass.

4 Go through a gate with tall slate slabs as supports. Continue towards Cove Road, **ignoring** a bridleway to the left to *Langscar Gate*. Long descent on grass then grass and stone. Go through the gate and turn **L** uphill on the road.

5 After 1km and just before the cattle grid turn **L** uphill through a gate onto a faint grassy track. After 300m at a fork of grassy tracks bear **R** alongside the wall. Soon join a new stone track for the next 6km. Great views of Pen-y-ghent and Ingleborough.

6 Descend. At the road turn **L** and immediately **L** again through a gate onto a track signposted *Bridleway to Settle*. Mainly grassy descent through gates then a steep stone downhill. Join tarmac and turn **L** to descend down to the square in the centre of Settle.

◄💬 Making a day of it

Take the bridleway from the northeast corner of the ride on the lane above Malham Cove across to Watersinks and Street Gate (GR 905 656) and you have all the *Mastiles Lane* rides to choose from – *see pages 7, 73 & 97*. Or instead of descending to Settle, link to the *Stainforth* ride – *see page 123* – and head northeast from Stainforth to Littondale.

MALHAM TARN

Kirkby Malham, Malham Tarn & Weets Top

23.6km

Introduction

'A ride of two halves'. The western half is all on quiet lanes from Calton and Airton north to Malham Tarn, the eastern half is almost entirely off-road from Malham Tarn south to Calton. The woodland surrounding Malham Tarn is remarkably lush considering the altitude (380m), indeed the whole setting of a lakeside trail within the boundaries of the Yorkshire Dales National Park is unusual. The ancient sheep drove of Mastiles Lane is justifiably one of the most popular off-road trails in the Dales and features in several rides. South of Mastiles Lane, it's three cheers for the National Park for the work they've done on the track over Calton Moor from Weets Top – you can't come down this without a grin.

The Ride

A long tarmac intro on lanes amid some of the finest scenery in the Dales takes you north through the hotspot of Malham and steeply up past Malham Cove to Malham Tarn and the start of the off-road, at first on some of the easiest in the book, around the wooded shores of the lake. After Street Gate and the beginning of Mastiles Lane the going gets more challenging. Take care not to miss the unsigned turn off south from Mastiles Lane towards Middle Laithe Farm and the only short section of tarmac in the eastern half of the ride. Climb steeply off-road to Weets Top and enjoy the tremendous downhill glide on improved track then grass then stone zig-zag to Calton where lanes finish the ride back to Kirkby Malham.

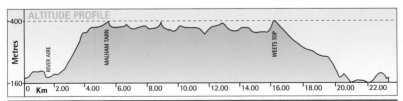

ALTITUDE PROFILE

Metres

400

160

RIVER AIRE

MALHAM TARN

WEETS TOP

0   Km   2.00   4.00   6.00   8.00   10.00   12.00   14.00   16.00   18.00   20.00   22.00

KIRKBY MALHAM, MALHAM TARN & WEETS TOP   GRADE:

DISTANCE: 23.6KM

TOTAL ASCENT: 550M

START/FINISH: KIRKBY MALHAM, NORTHWEST OF GARGRAVE

GRID REFERENCE: 895 610

PARKING: CAR PARK OFF THE LANE LEADING FROM THE VICTORIA PUB TOWARDS THE CHURCH

CAFÉ: OLD BARN CAFE, MALHAM Tel: 01729 830486

PUBLIC HOUSE: THE VICTORIA, KIRKBY MALHAM. BUCK INN, MALHAM

Kirkby Malham, Malham Tarn & Weets Top

Directions – Kirkby Malham, Malham Tarn & Weets Top

1 Follow the road for 2km north from Kirkby Malham up over the hill into Malham. At the fork of roads by the Buck Inn in Malham bear **L** signposted *Arncliffe*.

2 Follow this lane for 4.5km, climbing steeply past Malham Cove then more gently past Langscar Gate (cattlegrid). At the X-roads (GR 879 664) go **SA** signposted *Arncliffe*. At the next T-junction bear **R** signposted *Arncliffe*.

3 After 800m, and soon after the start of the trees on the right turn **R** on a tarmac lane by a *Malham Tarn National Trust* signpost. Pass around the back of the Field Centre to continue in the same direction.

4 Stay on the main stone track close the tarn. Go through a gate in a wall and follow the stone track as it bears **L** away from the tarn (**ignore** a *Pennine Way, Water Sinks Gate* sign pointing right onto a grassy track). After 800m, at the road turn **L** towards a gate in the wall and pass through the gate onto a stone and earth track signposted *Kilnsey* (GR 905 656).

5 After 600m drop to cross a ford then climb. **Very easy to miss:** almost 2km after this ford, at the bottom of a gentle dip with a gate 100m ahead and gates to the right and left in the enclosing wall, turn **R** onto an earth track climbing alongside a wire fence (no sign, GR 930 655).

6 After 1km and about 200m before the descent to Middle Laithe Farm (ahead of you and to the left) turn **R** through a gate onto a similar broad stone track, soon joining tarmac and descending with the farm to your left. **Easy to miss: ignore** the first lane to the left signposted *Footpath*. Shortly after the summit take the next wide stone track to the **L** signposted *Bridleway to Weets Top* (GR 924 635).

7 At the summit bear **R** signposted *Bridleway to Calton*. Dream descent on recently improved track. Go through a gate onto a grassy track, at times faint. Continue in the same direction, generally downhill for almost 1.5km to join a much clearer stone and grass and track zig-zagging downhill towards the woodland.

8   Descend to cross the stream bed then climb to Calton. Join tarmac and continue **SA**. Shortly, at a T-junction with a white line across the road, bear **R** (in effect **SA**) sign-posted *Airton*.

9   Descend to cross the River Aire and climb to Airton. At the 'green' bear **R** then at the T-junction turn **R** and follow the road for 2km north to Kirkby Malham back to the start.

◄⚙ Making a day of it

The ride from *Gargrave* passes through Airton – *see page 73*. The lane climb up above Malham Cove links to the *Settle* ride via Gorbeck – *see page 55*. The *Kilnsey* and *Grassington* rides also use Mastiles Lane – *see pages 7 & 97*.

THE GOOD, THE BAD AND THE UGLY

Embsay, Bolton Abbey & Embsay Moor

30km

Introduction

Tucked right into the southeast corner of the Yorkshire Dales National Park this ride even gives you the chance to soak up a bit of culture in the form of the architectural glories dotted around the valley north of Bolton Abbey. Shaped roughly like a figure of 8 on its side, the southern and western sections are all tarmac and the northern section all off-road. By starting at Embsay and mixing and matching, the stretches on tarmac are split into three, giving the ride more interest. The long off-road blast over Barden Moor/Embsay Moor offers some of the finest plateau cruising in the Dales, rolling through an expanse of heather with views over the Lower and Upper Barden Reservoirs.

The Ride

Climb up from Embsay, at times steeply, through Eastby and up onto Halton Moor to the cattlegrid, which is the point where the eastern and western loops touch. The grassy descent towards Bolton Abbey is steep and rutted in places, flattening out and becoming bumpy as it heads towards Westy Bank Wood, where it gets a little twistier and faster, although it's over too soon. Tarmac takes you to Halton East and the off-road climb back up to the cattlegrid. Now the real fun begins: enjoy one of the most beautifully set bridleways in the Dales, climbing 150m to the highpoint above Upper Barden Reservoir then dropping at times steeply down to the road at Rylstone. Be warned that the B6265 is fast and busy so put your heads down and go! go! go! to Brackenley Lane, leading back to Embsay.

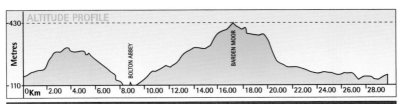

ALTITUDE PROFILE

Metres — 430 — 110

0 Km | 2.00 | 4.00 | 6.00 | 8.00 | 10.00 | 12.00 | 14.00 | 16.00 | 18.00 | 20.00 | 22.00 | 24.00 | 26.00 | 28.00

BOLTON ABBEY

BARDEN MOOR

EMBSAY, BOLTON ABBEY & EMBSAY MOOR   GRADE: ▲

DISTANCE: 30KM

TOTAL ASCENT: 690M

START/FINISH: EMBSAY, NORTH OF SKIPTON

GRID REFERENCE: 009 538

PARKING: CAR PARK AT THE EASTERN END OF THE VILLAGE

CAFÉ: BOLTON ABBEY

PUBLIC HOUSE: ELM TREE INN Tel: 01756 790717, CAVENDISH ARMS Tel: 01756 793980, BOTH IN EMBSAY

Embsay, Bolton Abbey & Embsay Moor

Directions – Embsay, Bolton Abbey & Embsay Moor

↪ With your back to the Elm Tree Inn in Embsay, turn **L**. Towards the end of the village turn **L** onto Kirk Lane signposted *Barden, Eastby.* Pass through Eastby, climb for 3km, at times steeply.

2 Shortly after the summit, with Lower Barden Reservoir in sight, and immediately after the cattle grid, turn **R** through the gate signposted *Bridleway to Bolton Abbey.* The good track becomes narrow, bumpy and grassy.

3 **Easy to miss:** about 3km after leaving tarmac, join a better track (used for access to the mast). About 100m after this, as the track swings sharp left towards the barn and the road (GR 062 553) turn **R** onto a faint grassy track towards a gate in the wall and the far woodland (Westy Bank Wood).

4 Enter the wood and follow the well-made gravel track through the trees. Exit the woodland, cross the field and go through the **left-hand** of the two gates. The track leads down to a tower by Bolton Hall. At the T-junction with the busy B6160 turn **R**, go through the arch then turn first **R** signposted *Village Hall, Post Office.*

5 **Easy to miss:** after 3km, shortly after the *30mph speed limit* signs at the start of the village of Halton East, and immediately after Halton Church Mission Room on the right, turn sharp **R** (GR 041 540). As the road swings left towards Calm Slate Farm continue **SA** uphill through a gate onto a stone and grassy track.

6 At the X-roads with the road by the cattlegrid go **SA** uphill onto the broad track opposite signposted *No motorised vehicles allowed.* Wonderful path on excellent surface through heather with Lower Barden Reservoir to the right.

7 After almost 2km at a T-junction of tracks (GR 023 561), with a stone shelter/shooting hut 200m up to the left, turn **R**.

8 Climb to the summit. **Ignore** a track off to the right to a second reservoir (Upper Barden) with a *No cycling* sign. About 1km after this turn, at another *No cycling* sign (GR 997 572), this time across the main track, turn **R** onto a new yellow stone banked-up track signposted *Bridleway.*

9 After 1.5 km, at the end of the improved section, join a wider more defined track. After a further 1.3km, at the T-junction with a good stone track (GR 973 577) turn **R** signposted *Bridleway to Rylstone*.

10 At the T-junction with the very busy B6265 turn **L**. To minimise time shared with traffic, the 5km you have to spend on this road should be ridden fast and in single file.

11 Ignoring farm drives, take the first proper lane to the **L** (Brackenley Lane) signposted *Memorial Woodland Burial Ground*. At the T-junction at the end of Brackenley Lane turn **L** to return to the start in Embsay.

◀☙ Making a day of it

Lying close to Rylstone at the west end of this ride, Hetton is on both the *Gargrave* and *Grassington* rides – *see pages 73 & 97*.

Gargrave to Mastiles Lane & Hetton

30.3km

Introduction

There's a real sense of linking lowland to highland in this ride. The starting point, Gargrave, lies on the busy A65 trunk road and has the Leeds & Liverpool Canal running through it; by contrast, the track known as Mastiles Lane at the north end of the ride is right in the heart of the Dales, running from Malham Tarn to Kilnsey Crags and climbing to over 400m through typical dales scenery of limestone crags. The change from lush pastures to moorland comes after Calton. The National Park has excelled itself once again around Weets Top laying down a fine stone track across what used to be a boggy mess. After a brief spell on Mastiles Lane, the ride turns south with a fine fast off-road descent to Hetton.

The Ride

Cross the Leeds & Liverpool Canal and climb gently northwest from Gargrave on an easy track through a gentle landscape of pasture and woodland. Pass through largely agricultural land as far as Airton, drop to cross the River Aire then face the major climb of the day, 250m on a mixture of tarmac (to Calton), stone track, faint grassy track, then improved track to reach Weets Top. A short, fast descent leads to Mastiles Lane, part of an ancient east–west drovers' route. Follow this briefly before turning off southeast, with the route linking the farmsteads at Bordley and Lainger House. Climb on tarmac after the bizarrely located telephone box then enjoy a long, ever-improving off-road downhill to Hetton. Lanes lead back to Gargrave.

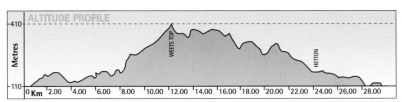

ALTITUDE PROFILE

GARGRAVE TO MASTILES LANE & HETTON

GRADE:

DISTANCE: 30.3KM

START/FINISH: GARGRAVE, ON THE A65 WEST OF SKIPTON

PARKING: FREE CAR PARK IN GARGRAVE

CAFÉ: DALESMAN CAFE, GARGRAVE (WALLS COVERED WITH CYCLING PHOTOS)

PUBLIC HOUSE: THE ANGEL, HETTON Tel: 01756 730263

TOTAL ASCENT: 645M

GRID REFERENCE: 934 453

**Gargrave to
Mastiles Lane & Hetton**

Directions – Gargrave to Mastiles Lane & Hetton

➎ With your back to the village hall in Gargrave turn **R** then on a sharp right-hand bend bear **L** onto West Street signposted *Leeds & Liverpool Canal, Pennine Way*. Shortly, on the next right-hand bend bear **L** onto Mark House Lane (no through road). Tarmac turns to track after 1km.

2 After 2km follow the track around a sharp left-hand bend with a barn (Crag Laithe) ahead. Rejoin tarmac on the next right-hand bend by the drive for Hesper (Espber) Farm. At the T-junction with the road turn **L** to cross the bridge over Otterburn Beck then turn immediately **R** signposted *Bell Busk*.

3 After 200m and shortly after a left-hand bend turn **R** through a gate onto a track between buildings signposted *Bridleway* (GR 903 566). Shortly after crossing a small stone bridge and passing a stone barn bear **L** off the stone track onto a grassy track alongside the fence. Go through a gate and bear **R** along the next field edge.

4 Continue in the same direction through several gates, past a barn on an ever more defined track. At the second barn the track becomes smooth stone and gravel. Go past a farm (Kirk Syke) on the left, climb gently to the road and bear **L**.

5 At the T-junction by a triangle of grass turn **R** then shortly at the X-roads with a more major road go **SA** signposted *Calton, Winterburn*. Descend to cross the River Aire then climb.

6 On a sharp right-hand bend bear **L** onto a no through road. Go through the hamlet of Calton and continue **SA** as tarmac turns to track, soon dropping to cross a ford then bearing **R** at a fork of tracks.

7 At the gate at the exit of woodland follow the sign *Bridleway to Weets Top* as the stone track swings **L** and steepens. Zig-zag up to a grassy track (at times faint) across moorland in a generally NNE direction. After 1.5 km arrive at the start of the improved track which you follow uphill for 2.5km.

8 At the top of the climb by a trig point (Weets Top) and a three-way signpost continue **SA** towards *Hawthorns*. Fast descent to the road. At the T-junction turn **R** then after 800m as the road/track swings right towards Middle Laithe Farm bear **L** (in effect **SA**) signposted *Mastiles Lane*. At the fork of tracks shortly after the farm take the right-hand gate (no sign).

9 After 1km at the T-junction with Mastiles Lane turn **R**. After 1km at a gate with a stone and cement cairn with a *No vehicles* sign and a stone barn with a low rusted roof to the left turn **R** by a 3-way signpost onto a faint grassy track alongside the wall (GR 937 657).

10 After 1km at a 4-way signpost at the start of tarmac turn **R** signposted *Bridleway to Bordley*. The track turns to tarmac near the summit. At the bottom of the descent turn **L** after the first stone barn through gates onto a track signposted *Bridleway to Boss Moor* and follow this for 2km.

11 Join tarmac by a farm (Lainger House) and a telephone box. Climb steeply on lane for 800m. Shortly after the summit, on a sharp left-hand bend just before the cattlegrid bear **R** downhill through a gate onto a walled track, a bit trashed by scramble bikes.

12 At a 5-way signpost (GR 951 608) continue **SA** down the *Bridleway to Hetton* on a fast descent to the road and turn **R** through the village.

13 After 3.5km, at a T-junction bear **L** (in effect **SA**) signposted *Gargrave*. Follow for a further 1.5km to return to the start.

◄●⊃O Making a day of it

The most obvious and satisfying extension would be to arrive at Mastiles Lane and turn left instead of right, follow the *Kilnsey* ride – see page 7 – round to Arncliffe Cote and back to Mastiles Lane to rejoin this ride.

DESCENDING FROM OLD COTE MOOR

Buckden & Littondale

20.3km

Introduction

The hillsides rise steep and high from this part of Wharfedale – to over 600m on the west side and over 700m on the east side. This ride crosses and recrosses Old Cote Moor Top to the west of the valley, starting from the compact village of Buckden, complete with pub and tearoom. Of the two crossings, the first is longer, steeper and rougher with some welcome paving slabs over the highest and boggiest parts of the summit. The descent to Littondale starts loose and rough and becomes grassier lower down the slopes. The climb back over to Wharfedale is less boggy and ends with a wonderful drop down into Kettlewell, nestling in the valley below.

The Ride

The climb from Buckden is amongst the toughest in the Dales with boggy conditions higher up – best avoided in winter! Slabs have been laid near the top, making for easier going over the wettest, softest ground, but it's still tricky. The descent has some technical sections with loose rock and steep slopes. The rock turns to grass and the gradient eases as you drop to the valley floor. A blast along the road leads to the return climb, which starts on a very steep bit of track, which soon flattens as it crosses the moorland, although it gets no easier. The descent is long, steep and loose, except for the washed-out slabs of limestone, which are short, flat and slippery. Be warned! Drop into Kettlewell and then spin back to Buckden.

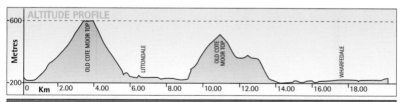

BUCKDEN & LITTONDALE

GRADE: ▲

DISTANCE: 20.3KM **TOTAL ASCENT:** 820M

START/FINISH: CAR PARK IN BUCKDEN, ON THE B6160 NORTH OF GRASSINGTON

PARKING: PAY & DISPLAY CAR PARK IN BUCKDEN. **GRID REFERENCE:** 943 774

CAFÉ: LOTS OF CHOICE IN KETTLEWELL. WEST WINDS TEAROOM, BUCKDEN Tel: 01756 760883 (OPEN TUES-SUN, EASTER TO END OF OCTOBER). RAIKES COTTAGE, ARNCLIFFE Tel: 01756 770240 (OPEN SAT-SUN EASTER TO END OF SEPTEMBER)

PUBLIC HOUSE: BUCK INN, BUCKDEN Tel: 01756 760228. QUEENS ARMS, LITTON Tel: 01756 770208. FALCON, ARNCLIFFE. LOTS OF CHOICE IN KETTLEWELL

Buckden & Littondale

p123 Stainforth to Littondale

p19 Tough Circuit above Kettlewell

Directions – Buckden & Littondale

5 Turn off the B6160 in Buckden on the lane heading northwest signposted *Hubber-holme, Hawes*. After 800m cross the bridge over the River Wharfe then shortly, by a *Redmire Farm* sign on a stone slab turn **L** signposted *Bridleway to Litton*. At the fork after the cattle grid bear **R** (Redmire Farm lies to the left).

2 Climb steeply on a broad, loose stone track zig-zagging up the hillside. Go through a gate near a small barn. After 300m at a 2-way signpost turn **R** off the main track onto a grassy track signposted *Bridleway* (GR 934 768).

3 Climb on the well-defined grassy path waymarked by blue-topped wooden stakes. As the gradient eases towards the summit after a very steep and boggy section, the bridleway runs over broad flat stones. Shortly after passing two stone cairns, the path jinks **L** then **R** through the wall, which is now to your right (GR 926 753).

4 More slabs at the start of the descent which then becomes steep with loose stones. The gradient eases and becomes grassier. Go through lots of gates and join tarmac beyond the farm. At the road by the Queens Arms pub in Litton turn **L** for 3.5km.

5 **Easy to miss:** go past a distinctive rock outcrop up to the left then shortly after the start of a cluster of houses on the edge of Arncliffe turn **L** by a *Bridleway to Starbotton* signpost onto a tarmac/stone track (GR 930 722).

6 Climb on a very steep concrete and grass track which ends just below Brayshaw Scar. At the fork of tracks shortly after passing through a wall opening, with the left-hand track heading towards a low stone barn with a green door, bear **R** up through heather aiming towards the right-hand end of the escarpment up ahead.

7 Climb to the highpoint. **Easy to miss:** on the descent as the path bears diagonally right across a field down towards a bridlegate in a well-maintained wall, turn sharp **R*** on a more level track towards another gate and another signpost, aiming towards the farm buildings and trees of Moor End. Follow the track up and around the farm.

8 Long generally excellent descent with one challenging section of steep rubble and wash out. At the road (B6160) turn **L** for 6.5km through Kettlewell then Starbotton to return to Buckden.

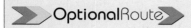

OptionalRoute

*Option B:
Instead of turning sharp right through the gate and onto the final descent, go **SA** through the gate ahead, following the bridleway around to the **L**, onto a very slippery, rocky and technical descent. Follow the bridleway down to a bridge. Go **SA** over the bridge and up to the gate, into Starbotton. Turn **L** and follow the road (B6160) to Buckden. If you can clean that descent you deserve a pint or two!

⚠️ **Safety Note:** This option is often popular with walkers and can be **very** slippery in the wet, when it becomes mega-technical. It also has a big drop off to one side... **Take care**.

Making a day of it

A short but very tough ride starts from *Kettlewell* – *see page 19*. The lane section down Litton-dale overlaps with the ride over from *Stainforth* – *see page 123*. Southeast from Arncliffe it is easy to link to the *Kilnsey–Mastiles Lane–Arncliffe Cote* ride – *see page 7*. Other rides nearby to the north are covered in this book's companion guide: **Yorkshire Dales Mountain Biking – The North Dales**.

WREAKS LANE

West of **Kirkby Malzeard**

30km

Introduction

Kirkby Malzeard, with its fine broad main street, is as far east as the rides go in this book – further east and you are in the Vale of York. The ride is not unlike the one starting from Masham climbing up from lush pastures, broadleaf woodland and fields of corn onto the heather grouse moors high above Nidderdale. Most of the height is gained on tarmac at the start of the ride climbing high onto Fountains Earth Moor. If you can face the climb back up, there are pubs to the west down in Nidderdale at Ramsgill and Lofthouse – you may use this as an excuse to extend the ride up towards Scar House Reservoir. A second climb north towards High Ash Head Moor takes you to the highest point on the ride and a big open blast across the heather back down to the start.

The Ride

The first section of off-road is one of those secret tracks it would be so easy to sail past, a little gem that drops to cross two tributaries of the River Laver before rejoining tarmac. Climb west onto Fountains Earth Moor and the views suddenly open up ahead down into Nidderdale and across to the hills beyond. Stop yourself on the plunge down towards Bouthwaite and turn north uphill alongside Lul Beck, climbing to join the well-made broad, stone-based track for an easy fast zoom back across Grewelthorpe Moor linking to the lane network west of Kirkby Malzeard.

Warning: *An obvious bridleway enters Kirkby Malzeard from the northwest. Don't bother with it. It starts well and ends well but the middle section is a series of muddy fields, gates, overgrown tracks and no signs.*

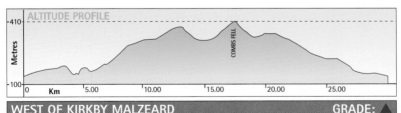

| ALTITUDE PROFILE | | | | | |

Metres: 410 / 100

Km: 0, 5.00, 10.00, 15.00, 20.00, 25.00

COMBS FELL

WEST OF KIRKBY MALZEARD

GRADE: ▲

DISTANCE: 30KM

TOTAL ASCENT: 420M

START/FINISH: KIRKBY MALZEARD, NORTHWEST OF RIPON

GRID REFERENCE: 230 743

PARKING: IN THE MAIN STREET OF KIRKBY MALZEARD.

CAFÉ: BRING SANDWICHES

PUBLIC HOUSE: HENRY JENKINS INN, KIRKBY MALZEARD Tel: 01765 658557

SE

14   15   16   Ilton Moor   17   18

Tower

Round Hill

West Summer Side

Agill

Shortlick Hill

p91 West from Masham

7

High Ash Head

76

Low Ash Head Moor

Arnagill

359 Sandy Hill

Cat Gill

ead Moor

375

Arnagill Moor

Foul Sike

Carle Tower

75

Combs Fell

299

Kirkby Malzeard Moor

342

300

Wansey Gill

p91 West from Masham

6

Summer Edge

414

enny & Tib Twigg

74

Typeland Crags

Lulbeck Crags

Carle Moor

ntaine Earth

p141 Pateley Bridge northwest

Hambleton Dike

Fortress Dike

4

300

73

Dalton Lodge

Glen View

Lulbeck Crags

375

North Gill Beck

5

72

375

p141 Pateley Bridge northwest

Kettlestang Hill

South Gill Beck

.295

Gate C

71

High Lathe

Byerbeck Gill

389

Sigsworth Moor

Jordan Moss

The Fleet

300

Fleet Seaves

Light Hill

.368

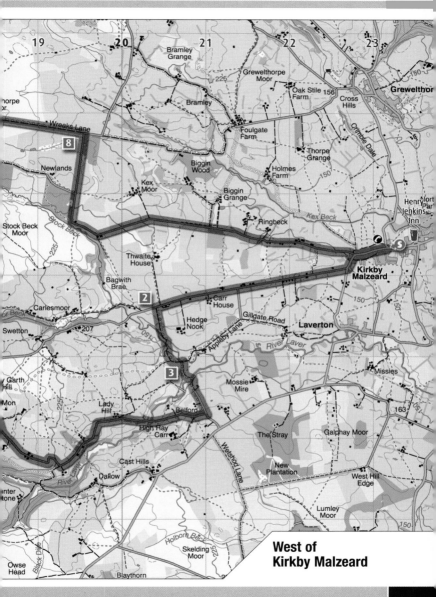

**West of
Kirkby Malzeard**

Directions – West of Kirkby Malzeard

⟹ From the centre of Kirkby Malzeard follow signs for *Dallowgill, Pateley Bridge*. About 200m after the end of the village turn **R** on the road signposted *Dallowgill*.

2 **Easy to miss:** after 2.5km and shortly after the summit of the second climb go past a roadside cottage on the left with arrow slit windows (Greystone Edge) then past a drive on the right to Thwaite House Farm and take the next track to the **L** signposted *Unsuitable for motors* (GR 204 736).

3 Fine track. Cross the stream via the ford or footbridge. **Ignore** a bridleway sign pointing right up alongside the field edge. Go through a heavy gate on a well-defined track and shortly turn **R** onto a similar track by an unusual mosaic down to your right. Climb, join tarmac and take the first road to the **R** (GR 210 722).

4 After 4km on this lane, on a sharp right-hand bend by a yellow stone house turn **L** uphill signposted *Unsuitable for motors* (GR 181 726). The tarmac ends after 2.4km, shortly after crossing the bridge.

5 **Easy to miss:** almost 2km after the summit, on a long descent, shortly after going through a gate, with an *Unsuitable for motors* sign ahead, turn **R** on the first major stone track (GR 135 718), climbing alongside the wall. Go past the conifer plantation to your left and at the fork of tracks, both with gates, bear **R** onto the upper track.

6 At the T-junction at the summit turn **R**. Fast descent then gentle climb through fields of heather.

7 At a fork of major tracks (GR 174 761) after almost 4km bear **R** (to the left the track leads towards forestry). Shortly, at the next fork stay on the main **left-hand** track (the right-hand track has heather growing down the middle).

8 Long fast descent. At the T-junction with the road on a sharp bend turn **R** signposted *Kirkby Malzeard*. Follow this lane for 4km into Kirkby Malzeard. At the road junction in Kirkby Malzeard go **SA** to return to the start.

◄💬 Making a day of it

Link either to the *Masham* ride – *see page 91* – which also crosses Masham Moor, or to the ride northwest from *Pateley Bridge* up to Scar House Reservoir – *see page 141*.

FREYA BLOOR AND PETE DODD

West from **Masham** towards **Nidderdale**

31km

Introduction

This is one of those lowland/highland routes or perhaps a more apt description for the Yorkshire Dales would be wood-land/moorland. It links the handsome town of Masham with its fine square and brewery via the gentle, lush and wooded scenery of the valley formed by the River Burn to the high heather moorland at over 400m on Masham Moor and Grewelthorpe Moor. The ride gains all its height on tarmac, travelling southwest into the prevailing winds, leaving you with a dream return leg on fine tracks and, with any luck, some wind assistance.

The Ride

Head west from Masham, hunting out the off-road tracks, the first and second of which are broad and stone-based. West of the River Burn crossing towards Leighton is a summer-only option, that crosses several fields – mudbaths in winter. The road through Fearby and Healey is an alternative. Climb on tarmac to the highpoint of the ride, pass Leighton Reservoir and drop to cross Agill Beck before resuming the climb. You are now set up nicely for a predomi-nantly downhill, wind-behind-you 15km ride, dropping over 300m. There are a few undulations across the heather-clad moor-land as you follow the shooting tracks at sonic-boom speeds. Ilton marks the return to civilisation and a trickier-to-follow track to the Swinton estate. A tarmac finish brings you back to Masham.

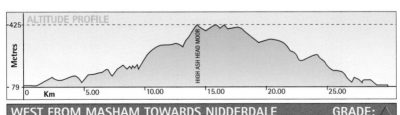

ALTITUDE PROFILE

HIGH ASH HEAD MOOR

WEST FROM MASHAM TOWARDS NIDDERDALE	GRADE: △
DISTANCE: 31KM	**TOTAL ASCENT:** 650M
START/FINISH: MASHAM	**GRID REFERENCE:** 225 807
PARKING: IN THE MAIN SQUARE IN MASHAM	
CAFÉ: LOTS OF CHOICE IN MASHAM	**PUBLIC HOUSE:** LOTS OF CHOICE IN MASHAM

West from Masham towards Nidderdale

p85 West from Kirkby Malham

Directions – West from Masham towards Nidderdale

❺ From the petrol station on the A6108 in Masham follow the road west towards Leyburn. At the end of the village turn **L** signposted *Leighton Reservoir, Fearby*.

2 After 2.4km go past Micklebury Farm and haybarns to the left and about 400m after the start of the climb turn **L** uphill on the first obvious broad stone track (GR 203 812, no sign). At the road bear **L** (in effect **SA**) then after 300m, on a left-hand bend, turn sharp **R** onto a similar broad stone track.

3 At the T-junction with the next road turn **L**. Go steeply downhill, cross the bridge over the River Burn then at the next T-junction turn **R** uphill signposted *Ilton*. After 500m, on a sharp left-hand bend bear **R** (in effect **SA**) onto a no through road signposted *Bridleway, Broadmires*.

4 Shortly, the tarmac turns to track. Go past Broadmires Farm and continue in same direction through a gate into field. The waymarking for the next section is a yellow arrow set in the outline of a yellow sun. Go through several gates and fields. The next 1.5km may be tough in winter when soft.

5 Eventually descend on the main track as it zig-zags down to cross a bridge over Pott Beck (GR 166 794). Bear **R** uphill on a grass track through ferns. Go through a gate then immediately after the dilapidated barn turn **R** through a gate into the next field. Aim diagonally uphill to a gate in the far corner of the field by the farm buildings of Leighton Hall. Go through this gate and the next one, turn **R** on the farm drive then **L** at the road.

6 Follow the road for almost 7km: go past Leighton Reservoir, climb, descend to cross Agill Beck then climb steeply. About 650m after crossing the cattlegrid at the summit, turn first **L** onto a broad smooth gravel track (GR 115 750) to go past a *Pott Moor High Road* signboard. At a fork soon after the gate take the upper **left-hand** stone track (a wide grass track leads down to the right).

7 After 2km, a track joins from the right by a boundary stone (GR 141 748). Gentle descent, gentle climb over the next 3km. About 700m after the summit, on the second gentle descent, as the conifer plantation comes into sight in the fold of the valley to your left, turn **L** downhill at the fork of wide tracks (GR 175 761).

8 Fine descent on superb moorland track. Go through a gate into field. Tarmac starts at the drive to the farm on the right (Brandwith Howe). At the T-junction with the road by some houses and a triangle of grass turn **L**.

9 **Easy to miss:** after 300m, on the descent, turn **R** on the first tarmac lane signposted *Hill Top Farm*. At the farm jink **R** then **L** between barns and stables to continue in the same direction on a stone then grass track. Follow the main grassy track, soon aiming towards a cluster of stone ruins and a hay barn with a rusty roof. Go through the gate, keeping the buildings to your left.

10 At the road turn **L** then after 350m take the first road to the **R**, following the wall.

11 After 1.5km, ignore a left turn signposted *Fearby*. Take the next **L** opposite the gates to Swinton House signposted *Masham*. At the T-junction in Masham at the end of Swinton Terrace turn **L** signposted *Bedale* to return to the start.

◄⚙ Making a day of it

The crossing of Masham Moor is also used in the *Kirkby Malzeard* ride – *see page 85.* At its western end it links with the ride northwest of *Pateley Bridge* – *see page 141.*

CLIMBING UP MASTILES LANE

Grassington, Mastiles Lane & Hetton 32km

Introduction

Grassington is the National Park HQ and a tourist hotspot. Strange fact: to the northeast of Grassington there are no bridleways; to the west there are bucket-loads. Many of these are being repaired with a stone base to prevent damage from scramble bikes. Purists feel that it rather sanitises the experience, removing all technical interest. Others point out that, while it might make for 'dull' riding, it does at least allow you to ride, rather than wade through a bog carrying your bike. The occasional rough section reminds you how this ride would be without the improvements. Particularly notable as a result of the work is the fast descent from Weets Top down towards Winterburn Reservoir.

The Ride

Head west through Threshfield to move off-road at the end of Moor Lane, crossing Threshfield Moor. Then turn north, across Malham Moor Lane to a few challenges on the rocks poking up through the grass. Join the major stone highway known as Mastiles Lane and climb to the route's highpoint on Kilnsey Moor. Leave Mastiles Lane and link the remote farms at Bordley and Middle Laithe before a sharp climb to Weets Top. A vast panorama spreads out before you with the track weaving down the hillside to Winterburn Reservoir. Climb from the reservoir, drop swiftly on a stone track to Hetton and follow lanes to the final long off-road section. This has all sorts, from narrow stone tracks to a patch of rough moorland, recently rebuilt tracks and old established trails. Cross the River Wharfe to return to Grassington.

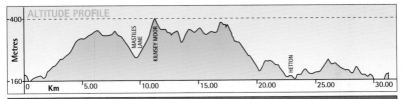

GRASSINGTON, MASTILES LANE & HETTON   GRADE:

DISTANCE: 32KM

TOTAL ASCENT: 675M

START/FINISH: GRASSINGTON

GRID REFERENCE: 003 637

PARKING: PAY & DISPLAY CAR PARK IN GRASSINGTON NEAR THE TOURIST INFORMATION CENTRE

PUBLIC HOUSE: LOTS OF CHOICE IN GRASSINGTON.

CAFÉ: LOTS OF CHOICE IN GRASSINGTON

ANGEL INN, HETTON Tel: 01756 730263. FOUNTAIN INN, LINTON Tel: 01756 752210

continues on
NEXT PAGE

p73 Gargrave to
Mastiles Lane & Hetton

Grassington, Mastiles Lane & Hetton (Part 1)

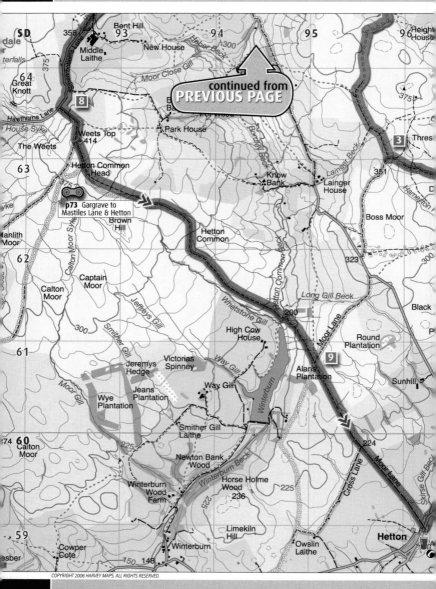

continued from
PREVIOUS PAGE

SD 93 356 Bent Hill 94 95 96

dale

terfalls 375 64 Great Knott

New House Heber Beck 300 Height House

Middle Laithe

Moor Close Gill

375

8 Hawthorns Lane House Syke

Weets Top 414 Park House

The Weets

63 Hetton Common Head

Brown Hill p73 Gargrave to Mastiles Lane & Hetton

Boss Moor

Hetton Common

62 Captain Moor Calton Moor

Calton Moor Syke

Jeffreys Gill

Smither Gill

Moor Gill

300

61 Jeremys Hedge Victorias Spinney

Wye Plantation Jeans Plantation

Way Gill

Way Gill

225

74 60 Calton Moor

Smither Gill Laithe

Newton Bank Wood

Winterburn Wood Farm

Winterburn Beck

Horse Holme Wood 236

Limekiln Hill

59 Cowper Cote Winterburn

150 148

esber

Park House
Forwood
Bordley Beck
Lainger Beck
Know Bank
Lainger House
351
Hamerton
323
300
Long Gill Beck
Whetstone Gill
Hetton Common Beck
200
Moor Lane
Round Plantation
9
Black
P
Sunhill
Alans Plantation
Winterburn
224
Moor Lane
Cross Lane
225
Owslin Laithe
Skirse Gill Beck
Hetton

High Cow House

Thres 3

Grassington, Mastiles Lane & Hetton (Part 2)

Directions – Grassington, Mastiles Lane & Hetton

→ From the centre of Grassington follow the B6265 towards Cracoe and Skipton, descending to cross the River Wharfe then climbing to Threshfield. At the T-junction with the B6160 turn **L** signposted *Skipton*. Descend to cross the bridge over Threshfield Beck, climb then take the first lane on the **R** (take care on this bend as the visibility is not good).

2 Tarmac turns to track. Go through a gate and at a fork (GR 975 630) turn **R** signposted *Bridleway* (straight ahead is a footpath to Cracoe & Winterburn). At the next fork bear **L** (there are grouse butts to the right).

3 Climb steadily over the next 1.5km on an improved track to a junction of tracks (GR 958 630) by a wooden waymark. Turn **R** signposted *Malham Moor Lane* on a continuation of the improved path. At the track junction by a *Footpath to Skirethorns* signpost continue **SA** through a gate onto a walled track. More excellent improved path over the next 2km.

4 At the road (Malham Moor Lane) go **SA** through the gate opposite signposted *Bridleway to Kilnsey*, following blue-topped wooden posts. Climb then descend over the next 3km on a rougher grassy track with stones poking up as you continue roughly north. There are several forks as the track splits then rejoins.

5 At the junction with a wide stone track between walls (Mastiles Lane) by gates and sheep pens turn **L** uphill. Climb to the summit, descend, then at the next gate and a 3-way signpost turn **L** signposted *Bridleway* onto a track running along a dry valley.

6 After 800m at a X-roads of tracks and a tarmac lane at a 4-way signpost go **SA** signposted *Bridleway to Bordley*. Go **SA** through Bordley Farm. Climb on a good stone and grass track then a good grass track. Descend on a zig-zag path to cross a dry valley (GR 932 650).

7 Climb, then at a T-junction with a broad track bear **R** (in effect go **SA**). About 100m before Middle Laithe Farm jink sharp **R** then sharp **L** onto a good track between walls. Join tarmac by the farm.

8   **Easy to miss:** ignore the first lane to the left signposted *Footpath*. Shortly after the summit take the next wide stone track to the **L** signposted *Bridleway to Weets Top*. At a 3-way signpost at the top of the climb bear **L** signposted *Bridleway to Hetton* on an improved path for the next 3km.

9   Descend to cross the stream feeding Winterburn Reservoir then climb. At a 5-way signpost at the top of the climb go **SA** signposted *Bridleway to Hetton*. Fast descent on broad stone track.

10   At the T-junction with the road in Hetton turn **L** downhill. **Ignore** turnings to right and left for 1.5km. Immediately before a *Give Way* sign in Cracoe near the junction with the B6265, turn **L** downhill onto a track signposted *Bridleway to Linton*.

11   Follow the broad stone and grass track under a railway bridge then after 600m, with gates left, right and straight ahead at the end of the broad path, turn **L** onto a narrower track between walls. At the end of the overgrown walled section continue **SA** across the field towards the barn on the skyline (GR 972 613).

12   From the barn go downhill towards the **right-hand** end of the copse of trees. Go through a bridlegate, cross a stream (Eller Beck) and climb steeply to join an excellent new stone track.

13   Go through gate onto a wide stone track. Cross the busy B6265 **SA** uphill onto a narrow track signposted *Bridleway to Linton*. Emerge onto a broad track by barns. Cross the railway bridge and at the B6265 bear **L** to go through the village of Linton.

14   At the X-roads with the B6160 go **SA** downhill signposted *Linton Falls*. At the T-junction turn **R** signposted *Grassington* to return to start.

◄⚙⚙⚙ **Making a day of it**

Try adding on the *Kilnsey* ride in reverse – *see page 7* – in other words, get to Mastiles Lane, turn right instead of left, drop down to Kilnsey then Arncliffe Cote–High Cote Moor–Street Gate–Mastiles Lane.

SECTION 3

Enduros

Now we're talking. Pack your sarnies and your chain lube. These are big, tough rides (for big, tough riders?) that'll probably take you all day. They're challenging routes for fit and experienced mountain bikers – you know – proper riding.

Riding where you might describe the route as 'a bit of a beast'.

Enduros
sponsored by **timeoutdoors**.com

www.timeoutdoors.com

MOORLAND CRUISING ABOVE MALHAM

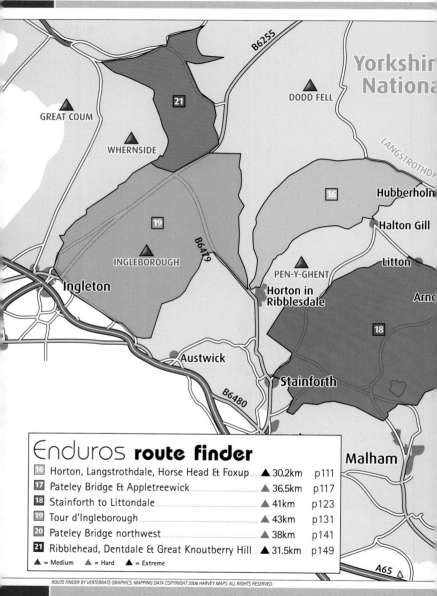

Enduros **route finder**

▲ = Medium   ▲ = Hard   ▲ = Extreme

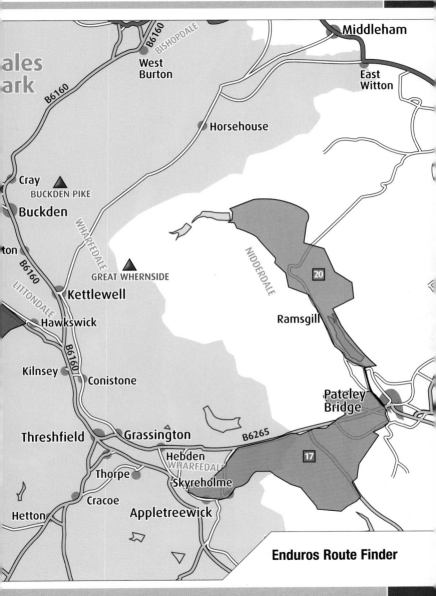

Enduros Route Finder

LEAVING HORTON

Horton, Langstrothdale, Horse Head & Foxup

30.2km

Introduction

If Horton is towards the edge of the National Park then Langstrothdale and Littondale are right in its very heart, surrounded by fells rising to over 600m. The outward route from Horton to Langstrothdale presents no real problems – a climb on the Pennine Way on a broad stone track then an easy forest section. The next stage could not be more different – the link from Langstrothdale to Littondale starts with the hardest, roughest and steepest climb in the book and ends with one of the best descents in the Dales. As if two climbs were not enough there is a final challenge out of Littondale across Foxup Moor beneath the great bulk of Pen-y-ghent.

The Ride

The climb north from Horton is all rideable. Join a forest track then a lane as you descend gently to Langstrothdale and the infant River Wharfe. From Raisgill to Horse Head you are faced with 360m of climbing in just over 2km, much of it unrideable. Arriving at the top, take stock of the 360° panorama and anticipate your reward – 300 vertical metres of descent in about 1.5km! At the bottom there is a chance of a beer just off the route in Litton before the last climb, up to the slopes beneath the summit of Pen-y-ghent on a track which has a bit of everything: grassy track, some improved trail, some boggy stuff and a broad loose stone section dropping you back into Horton.

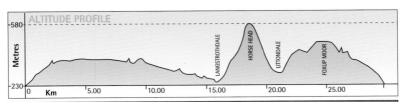

ALTITUDE PROFILE

Metres — 580 — 230

Km   5.00   10.00   15.00   20.00   25.00

LANGSTROTHDALE · HORSE HEAD · LITTONDALE · FOXUP MOOR

HORTON, LANGSTROTHDALE, HORSE HEAD & FOXUP   GRADE: ▲

DISTANCE: 30.2KM

TOTAL ASCENT: 909M

START/FINISH: HORTON IN RIBBLESDALE, ON THE B6479 NORTH OF SETTLE

PARKING: PAY & DISPLAY CAR PARK IN HORTON

GRID REFERENCE: 807 727

CAFÉ: THE PEN-Y-GHENT CAFE IN HORTON Tel: 01729 860333 (SHUT TUESDAYS)

PUBLIC HOUSE: GEORGE INN 2KM OFF THE ROUTE IN HUBBERHOLME Tel: 01756 760223.
QUEENS ARMS 3KM OFF THE ROUTE IN LITTON Tel: 01756 770208

SD 80 81 82 83 84 85

Arletree

Cam End

Cam Fell

Round Hill

Beckermc Scar

Round Hill

Low Green Field

ones

80

News Head Hill

High Green Field

Greenfield

Broad Reyn Hill

Scald Bank

Ling Gill Bridge

Low Green Field Knot

Tile Hill

79

Sike Moor

Cave Hill

Ely Hill

High Green Field Knott

602

Nether Lodge

Brongill Cave

Greenhaw Moor

Cosh Beck Head

Low Rigg

78

Lord's Seat

Old Ing

599

477.

510

Holme Hill

High Birkwith

2 Birkwith Moor

Scutching Close

77

Low Birkwith

Blaydike Moss

Foxup Road

76

Long Mires

Brown Hackeber Hill

Foxup Beck

8

witt Hill

Scale Farm

Green Hackeber Hill

Swarth Gill Gate

Foxup Moor

9

The Tarn

Jackdaw Hole

Penyghent Long Churn

Cross Pot

Todber Moss

Turpen

Horton Moor

Plover Hill

75

Top Farm

Whitber Hill

Hull Pot

681

665

Fawber

Sell Gill Holes

Hunt Pot

Pen-y-ghent Fell

Low Moor

74

▲

p131 Tour d'Ingleborough

w Houses

Horton Scar

Penyghent Pot

Pen-y-ghent

Pen

p131 Tour d'Ingleborough

Rowe Farm

73

Beecroft Hall

S Horton in Ribblesdale

10 Douk Ghyll Scar

Fawcett Moor

Pen-y-ghent Quarry

Pen-y-ghent Café

▲

Bracken-bottom

Larch Tree Hole

433

Rainscar

72

Horton, Langstrothdale, Horse Head & Foxup

p123 Stainforth to Littondale

Directions – Horton, Langstrothdale, Horse Head & Foxup

➎ Follow the B6479 through Horton towards Ribblehead and Hawes. At the north end of the village on a sharp left-hand bend turn **R** in front of the Crown pub through the front car park onto the Pennine Way.

2 After 5km at a fork of tracks where the Pennine Way goes left, bear **R** (GR 813 772). Soon join a better forest track/road and bear **R**. Join tarmac by High Green Field Farm. Follow this lane for 5km passing through several gates.

3 At the T-junction with the road through Langstrothdale turn **R** signposted *Buckden, Kettlewell* down the valley for 3.5km.

4 Cross the river at Deepdale Farm, go past a stone bridge on the left at Yockenthwaite, climb, then just before the first house on the right, turn **R** by a stone and concrete cairn signposted *Halton Gill* (GR 905 786).

5 The next 2.3km are very steep, and largely unrideable up to the summit (360m of ascent). This is followed by an absolutely fabulous descent from Horse Head down into Littondale.

6 At the road at the bottom turn **R** then after 800m and about 50m after the end of the tarmac, opposite the stone hump-backed bridge by Foxup Bridge Farm, turn **L** signposted *Bridleway to Horton in Ribblesdale*. At the gate that leads into a field with no obvious track bear **R** steeply uphill towards a gap in a stone wall and a wooden, blue-topped signpost (near a TV aerial). Go through a gate and continue in same direction.

7 Follow the direction of the signpost on a track parallel to the wall and at a distance of about 100m from it. After 800m it swings **R** on a more level course parallel with the ridge to the left.

8 After 1.2km of relatively flat riding, at a gate in the stone wall and a signpost with *Bridleway to Horton 4¼ miles*, bear steeply **L** uphill following the direction of the signpost (GR 855 763). Lots of fun tricky stone and grass to navigate.

9 There is a short section of improved yellow gravel path which starts soon after the footpath to Plover Hill (GR 846 761). The improved section ends and there is a rougher stretch of about 1.5km before the start of the descent on a broad stone track (GR 823 743).

10 After 2.5km at a fork near the bottom of the descent turn **R** then at the road turn **R** again to return to the start in Horton.

◄🔗 Making a day of it

You want more? This is one of the most central rides in the book with opportunities to link to the *Tour d'Ingleborough* – *see page 131* – the ride from *Stainforth* at Helwith Bridge – *see page 123* – and the *Buckden* ride at Litton – *see page 79*. North out of Langstrothdale there are links to rides featured in this book's companion guide: **Yorkshire Dales Mountain Biking – The North Dales**.

Pateley Bridge & Appletreewick 36.5km

Introduction

Nidderdale and Pateley Bridge lie outside the National Park. From a mountain biking angle there are excellent trails northwest from Pateley Bridge past the reservoirs all the way to Coverdale and to the west, featured here, trails lead to the fine little village of Appletreewick with a pub that welcomes mountain bikers. Highlights of the ride include a climb up through old lead mining ruins near Pateley, a 150m off-road descent down into Appletreewick with the odd tricky challenge, one of the finest climbs in the book up Skyreholme Bank onto Pock Stones Moor and a final off-road downhill using a grouse moor road over Flat Moor to Middle Tongue, just short of Pateley.

The Ride

Head northwest from Pateley, moving off-road alongside Ashfold Beck and climbing steeply through mining ruins. Cross two streams and climb to the B6265, joining it close to the summit. Descend past Stump Cross Caverns for a short spell along a lane leading to the stunning descent to Appletreewick and the bike-friendly New Inn. Lanes through the village lead to one of the best climbs in the book – a superb track beneath the distinctive rocky outcrops of Simon's Seat and Hen Stones. Cross Pock Stones Moor, descending from a highpoint of 430m to the road at 285m. A short road section leads to a boggy section for about 1km before sanity returns as you join a shooting track that drops to the road at Middle Tongue and the dark, wooded tarmac return to Pateley.

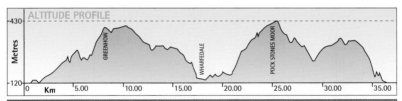

PATELEY BRIDGE & APPLETREEWICK   GRADE: ▲

DISTANCE: 36.5KM

START/FINISH: PATELEY BRIDGE

PARKING: PAY & DISPLAY IN PATELEY BRIDGE

TOTAL ASCENT: 1025M

GRID REFERENCE: 157 654

PUBLIC HOUSE: NEW INN, APPLETREEWICK Tel: 01756 720252

CAFÉ: TEAROOM AT PARCEVALL HALL, EAST OF APPLETREEWICK Tel: 01756 7203630 (OPEN APRIL TO SEPTEMBER).
STUMP CROSS CAVERNS CAFE Tel: 01756 752780

**Pateley Bridge
& Appletreewick**

Directions – Pateley Bridge & Appletreewick

➎ From the centre of Pateley Bridge, briefly follow the B6265 towards Grassington, cross the bridge over the River Nidd then shortly turn first **R** onto Low Wath Road signposted *Ramsgill, Upper Nidderdale*.

2 After 1.5km go past the Bridge Inn then take the first road to the **L** signposted *Heathfield* and shortly turn **L** again signposted *Heathfield Caravan Park, Bridleway*.

3 Go through several caravan sites following the main tarmac road, keeping **L** at forks. At the end of the tarmac follow the good stone track alongside the stream and through broadleaf woodland. Shortly after going through two closely spaced gates, with a *Private Road* sign ahead, bear **L** downhill signposted *Nidderdale Way* (GR 119 661), leaving the main track.

4 Cross the river (Ashfold Side Beck) and zig-zag up the hillside through ruins and spoil heaps – this is a bit confusing as there are several tracks. Soon join a good broad gravel and grass track going straight up the hillside, passing to the **R** of a summit of outcrops of stones. At a 3-way signpost continue **SA** downhill signposted *Bridleway to Pateley Bridge & Toft Gate*.

5 Keep following *Nidderdale Way* signs down to cross the stream then climb. At the T-junction with the road turn **L** by a *Roundhill Farm* sign (GR 131 653) then shortly take the first **R** sharply back on yourself on a tarmac and grass lane signposted *Toft Gate*. **Easy to miss:** after 200m and immediately **before** the cattlegrid bear **R** away from the stone track onto a grassy track towards a gate with a white sign on it.

6 At the T-junction with tarmac turn **L** to continue uphill then shortly at the T-junction with the B6265 turn **R**. Descend, climb, descend, passing the Miners Arms, a church, a mast and Stump Cross Caverns.

7 After 5.5km, shortly after the start of a climb following a long descent, take the first road to the **L** signposted *Appletreewick*. After 1.2km and soon after a sharp left-hand bend turn **R** through a gate signposted *Bridleway to Hartington*.

8 At the fork of tracks after 1.4km bear **R** to go through a gate onto a walled track (the left fork goes down to a barn). At the road turn **L** to go through Appletreewick.

9 Following signs for *Skyreholme and Pateley Bridge*, **ignore** a right turn signposted *Skipton, Bolton Abbey*. Climb and take the next **R** onto a no through road signposted *Skyreholme*.

10 At the T-junction with *Parcevall Hall* signposted to the left turn **R** to cross the bridge over Skyreholme Beck. Steady climb to the end of tarmac. At the junction of tracks (GR 078 616) as the left-hand track swings sharply uphill bear **R** signposted *No cars or motor bikes except for access*. Superb climb on excellent quality track.

11 Climb to the highpoint, descend to a stream crossing (Harden Gill), short climb then longer descent. At the road turn **L** downhill. Once again down then up, crossing the River Washburn.

12 At the T-junction at the end of Hoodstorth Lane turn **L** signposted *Pateley Bridge*. After 1km go past the drive to Humberstone Bank on the left then shortly turn **R** through a gate onto the drive towards High House Farm signposted *Bridleway*. Pass to the **L** of buildings, go through two gates and alongside the wall on the **right-hand** edge of the field.

13 The next kilometre is tough going! Go through the next gate (with the stones of Palleys Crags ahead) and turn **L** alongside wall on a very rough, barely visible track through reedy grass, following the occasional wooden post. Join a more distinct path by a signpost with blue arrows on a yellow background and turn **R** alongside the wall.

14 Join an excellent stone-based track leading through heather towards Pateley Bridge. Keep bearing **L** on an ever better track to descend to the road and turn **R** downhill. Follow the steep and very dark lane through woodland.

15 At the T-junction at the end of Peat Lane turn **L** downhill. Bear **R** at a fork of lanes down a hill signposted *1 in 7*. At the T-junction in Pateley turn **R** to return to the start.

◄━◯◯ Making a day of it

Another ride starts from *Pateley Bridge* heading northwest past the reservoirs – *see page 141*.

NICK COTTON KEEPING HIS FEET DRY

Stainforth to Littondale

Introduction

In the very heart of the Dales there are many top quality tracks which could be ridden in either direction and could be bolted together in all sorts of ways to make shorter or longer rides, going clockwise or anticlockwise. This ride is a case in point – it can easily be length-ened by going over Old Cote Moor to Kettlewell and Buckden. The ride itself is fairly long and fairly tough but the quality of the tracks is generally excel-lent, whether on the climb up towards Pen-y-ghent, the descent to Litton, the grassy climb over High Cote Moor or the newly improved trail over Gorbeck – every one a delight.

The Ride

An unforgiving tarmac climb from Stainforth sets you up for the first off-road section, starting easily and quickly turning into a loose and rocky descent. Turning right, you are faced with the bulk of Pen-y-ghent as you climb steadily back to a lane which you join briefly before an easy (but good) descent on a well-made track down to Littondale. The following climb from Arncliffe Cote is the longest and toughest of the day with a loose, stony start. After the grassy descent from the summit there is a quirky section along a streambed just before reaching Street Gate. Lane and track lead to the start of the unclassified road of Gorbeck, before a final tarmac climb and an off-road cruise brings you to a mighty descent right into the heart of Stainforth.

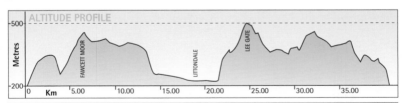

ALTITUDE PROFILE

Metres — 500, 200 | Km 5.00 10.00 15.00 20.00 25.00 30.00 35.00

FAWCETT MOOR · LITTONDALE · LEE GATE

STAINFORTH TO LITTONDALE   GRADE:

DISTANCE: 41KM

TOTAL ASCENT: 1042M

START/FINISH: STAINFORTH, ON THE B6479 NORTH OF SETTLE

GRID REFERENCE: 820 672

PARKING: FREE CAR PARK ON B6479

PUBLIC HOUSE: CRAVEN HEIFER, STAINFORTH Tel: 01729 822599. QUEENS ARMS, LITTON Tel: 01756 770208. FALCON, ARNCLIFFE. TENNANT ARMS, KILNSEY Tel: 01756 752301

CAFE: RAIKES COTTAGE, ARNCLIFFE Tel: 01756 770240 (OPEN SAT-SUN EASTER TO END OF SEPTEMBER)

continues on
NEXT PAGE

**Stainforth to Littondale
(Part 1)**

continued from
PREVIOUS PAGE

**Stainforth to Littondale
(Part 2)**

Directions – Stainforth to Littondale

➎ From the main car park in Stainforth (on the B6479 near to the church) follow the minor road northwest towards Halton Gill and Arncliffe. Shortly, on a sharp right-hand bend turn **L** signposted *Halton Gill, Arncliffe*.

2 After 2km, at the top of the second steep section, just before a descent to a farm (Sannat Hall), turn **L** onto an unsigned broad stone track between stone walls (by a telegraph pole). Follow the broad stone track through gates.

3 Rocky descent. At a T-junction with a similar broad stone track (GR 818 697) turn **R** signposted *Bridleway to Dale Head* and climb steadily.

4 The summit comes after 2.6km with Pen-y-ghent looming. Follow the main track as it swings right (southeast), go past the farm to the road and turn **L** over the cattlegrid.

5 Follow the road for 2km – climbing to the summit then, **easy to miss**, on the descent, bear **R** by a *No through road* signpost onto a stone and grass track (GR 855 729). Superb breezy track over the next 5km in excellent condition.

6 Fine descent, cross the bridge over the River Skirfare, then at the road turn **R** to go through Litton.

7 Follow the road down the valley into Arncliffe, recross the River Skirfare then at the T-junction in the village turn **L** signposted *Kilnsey, Grassington*. **Easy to miss:** after 2km take the first tarmac turn on the **R** signposted *Arncliffe Cote, Bridleway to Street Gate*.

8 Continue **SA** at the end of tarmac through a gate onto a steep and stony track. At the second gate follow the main grassy track round to the **R** alongside the wall, zig-zagging up the hillside. You soon come to a grassy fork – take either track as they both rejoin. The generally excellent grassy track splits on a few occasions but all options lead up to the highpoint which is roughly halfway between Arncliffe Cote and Street Gate (4km after leaving the road).

9 On the descent you will need to go through a shallow stream bed/ford but it is stone-based and rideable. Descend through a final gate and on to tarmac. Continue **SA** for 100m then at the junction with the road bear **R** signposted *Settle*.

10 After 1km, go past a car parking area on the right, cross a stream then turn **L** through a gate onto a grass track signposted *Bridleway to Langscar Gate*. Shortly bear **R** uphill at a fork by a *Langscar Gate* signpost.

11 At the road turn **L** to cross the cattle grid and turn immediately **R** through a gate, uphill onto a grassy track. After 300m at a fork of grassy tracks bear **R** alongside the wall. Soon join a superb new stone track for the next 6km (with one short unimproved section). Great views to the right to Pen-y-ghent and Ingleborough.

12 Descend, then at the T-junction with the road turn **R** uphill. After 800m, shortly after a cattlegrid, turn **L** downhill opposite a rock outcrop on the right onto a tarmac lane, crossing another cattlegrid.

13 At a X-roads of tracks by farm buildings (Upper Winskill) turn **R** signposted *Bridle-way, Catrigg Force* onto a stone and grass path alongside the wall. At the T-junction with a more defined path (GR 832 668) turn **L** downhill through a gate.

14 Superb steep descent with lots of gates. At the bottom keep bearing **L** then at the T-junction by the Craven Heifer pub turn **R** to return to the car park in Stainforth.

◄⊙⊙ Making a day of it

There are easy links to many rides: west from Litton to the *Horton–Langstrothdale* ride – *see page 111* – over Old Cote Moor Top on the *Buckden* ride – *see page 79* – from Street Gate to the various rides that use all or part of Mastiles Lane – *see pages 7, 73 & 97*.

PETE DODD THROWING SHAPES ON INGLEBOROUGH

Tour d'Ingleborough

43km

Introduction

Although there is a bridleway from Ingleton right to the top of Ingleborough it is a there-and-back route, unrideable at the top and full of walkers – avoid it at all costs. This is a far better alternative – a circuit around one of the famous Three Peaks linking three long off-road stretches via stunning road sections that just happen to go past several pubs and cafes in Clapham, Horton and Ribblehead. There are large slabs of Yorkshire Dales' trademark limestone pavement either side of the route on the way north from Clapham to Selside and back across Scales Moor. And let us not forget the tunnels north of Clapham...

The Ride

A lane section from Ingleton to Clapham warms you up with views south to the Bowland Hills. Clapham boasts several cafés in case you need a carb fix for the first major climb. Pass the church and follow a broad stone track through tunnels before climbing above woodland and onto the grassy plateau on Long Scar. Drop easily into Horton on tarmac and follow the lane to Old Ing, joining the Pennine Way and passing ancient woodland at Ling Gill. The Ribblehead Viaduct looms and you pass beneath it before picking up the bleak and often indistinct track across Scales Moor with Ingleborough away to the left. A belter of a descent down a grassy zig-zag takes you to the road and fast lanes back to Ingleton.

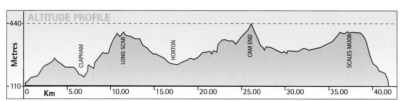

TOUR D'INGLEBOROUGH   GRADE:

DISTANCE: 43KM

START/FINISH: INGLETON

PARKING: SEVERAL PAY & DISPLAY CAR PARKS IN INGLETON

CAFÉ: LOTS OF CHOICE IN INGLETON. PEN-Y-GHENT CAFE IN HORTON Tel: 01729 860333

PUBLIC HOUSE: LOTS OF CHOICE IN INGLETON. NEW INN, CLAPHAM Tel: 015 242 51203.
CROWN INN, HORTON Tel: 01729 860209. STATION INN, RIBBLEHEAD Tel: 015 242 41274

TOTAL ASCENT: 700M

GRID REFERENCE: 695 733

continues on
NEXT PAGE

Tour d'Ingleborough (Part 1)

continued from PREVIOUS PAGE

p25 Ingleton, Kingsdale & North End Scar

**Tour d'Ingleborough
(Part 2)**

Directions – Tour d'Ingleborough

⑤► From the centre of Ingleton follow signs for Hawes. At the T-junction with the B6255 turn **L** then after 300m take the first road **R** signposted *Clapham*. Follow this road up and down for almost 6km with fine views right towards the Bowland Hills.

2 At the bottom of a fast descent on the edge of Clapham turn **L** onto Eggshell Lane (GR 743 686) signposted *Unsuitable for wide vehicles*. Shortly, **ignore** a lane to the right, descend towards the village and take the first road **L** (Church Lane) signposted *Austwick*. Cross the bridge, go past the church and immediately bear **L** onto a wide stone track which soon turns sharp **L** signposted *Bridleway to Austwick*.

3 Go through two tunnels. Shortly after the end of the steep section turn **L** onto a broad stone track signposted *No cars or motorbikes, Bridleway to Selside*. Steep down then up then a flat section to take you past a cave down to your left.

4 After a steep loose stone climb go through a gate then bear **R** on a smooth wide grassy track towards a cairn on the horizon (and a gate in the wall before this). Keep bearing **R** uphill to arrive at a square stone and cement cairn with a *No vehicles* sign on its far side. Turn **L** then shortly at the fork of tracks bear **R** towards a pyramid-shaped cairn.

5 Continue on a smooth flat grass track towards a second square stone and cement cairn (GR 773 724), passing beneath a tumbledown wall up to the left. At a 4-way signpost set on a stone and cement base go **SA** signposted *Selside*.

6 At the fork immediately after a gate with a *Please follow waymarks* sign on it, bear **L**. Shortly at the next fork bear **R** downhill following a series of low wooden posts with green waymarks. The grass track turns to stone then tarmac as you bear **L** to descend to the road. At the B6479 turn **R*** for 3km.

> * ►OR► for a short cut, turn **L** to go directly to Ribblehead and rejoin at **9**.

7 Follow the road through Horton towards Settle, cross the bridge over the River Ribble and just before the Crown pub turn **L*** onto a no through road leading past the pub car park.

> * ►OR► for the excellent Pen-y-ghent Café (tel: 01729 860333, shut Tuesdays) turn **R** towards the south end of Horton.

8 The tarmac ends after 5km at High Birkwith. Continue **SA** through a gate on a track signposted *Old Ing*. At a fork of tracks beyond the gate after passing a house on the right (Old Ing) turn **L.** Wonderfully improved track.

9 Cross a stone bridge over the stream and continue uphill. Climb on largely unrideable rough 'cobbled' brick-size stones. At the T-junction of tracks by a 3-way signpost turn **L** signposted *Dales Way*. Descend to cross the stream via bridge or ford. At the T-junction with the B6255 turn **L**.

10 About 50m before the Station Inn turn **R** into the car park by large boulders and head for the famous Ribblehead Viaduct. Follow the broad stone track underneath the viaduct. Continue on this track, keeping the Gunnerfleet Farm buildings to the right, cross a small bridge with a metal railing then at tarmac turn **R**.

Tour d'Ingleborough — continued

11 After a short climb, at the T-junction turn **L** signposted *Bridleway to Scar End*. Pass directly in front of an old farmhouse with five sash windows then bear **R** through two gates following the direction of the *Scar End* signpost, in other words, go into the field on the track and not on the upper right-hand tarmac drive towards a house.

12 **Easy to miss:** bear **R** by a post towards a yellow marker by a narrow bridlegate in a wall. Route finding is a bit confusing but basically continue in the same southwesterly direction through a series of bridlegates on grassy tracks passing several farm out-buildings. At a *Scar End 3¼, Deepdale 7¾* signpost, as the main track swings left continue **SA** on a rougher stone and grass track (GR 731 784).

13 The next 5km across Scales Moor is a bit vague and almost entirely without waymarking. Basically follow the reasonably distinct grassy track over moorland at the foot of the escarpment to the right. After about 3km and shortly after passing a wooden post near a section of limestone pavement jink **L** then **R** to continue in the same direction as previously. You are heading towards the pyramid-shaped cairn equidistant from two square stone windbreaks, passing through a shallow stone gully cut through the limestone pavement.

14 Descend on a zig-zag grass and stone track with fabulous views. Join a better stone track and bear **L**. Go through a gate, the track turns to tarmac and follow the lane as it swings **R** downhill between buildings. Join a wider road at a second gate and bear **R** to continue downhill. At the T-junction in Ingleton at the end of Mill Lane turn **L** to climb back up into the centre of Ingleton.

◀ ⚙️ Making a day of it

Another ride starts from Ingleton, heading north up into Kingsdale – *see page 25*. There are links to two other rides: from *Clapham to Austwick and Feizor* – *see page 31* – and from *Horton to Langstrothdale* – *see page 111*. A ride north from Ribblehead is covered on *page 149*.

LOFTHOUSE MOOR

Pateley Bridge northwest

Introduction

One of the classic rides of the Yorkshire Dales, following the valley of the River Nidd northwest from Pateley Bridge past Gouthwaite Reservoir on a mixture of quiet lanes, easy tracks and tough challenges. The lower part of the ride passes through a lovely rolling countryside dotted with clumps of broadleaf trees and farms. A tough off-road climb takes you from Middlesmoor to high above Scar House Reservoir with a descent to challenge nerves and suspension. The return stays high above the valley with one severely steep climb out of the gully formed by the magically named Woo Gill and Twizling Gill. Fine tracks across grouse moors lead down to the valley floor for an easy finish to Pateley.

The Ride

A tarmac warm-up leads to the first off-road section: along the Nidderdale Way up above the valley. Rejoining the road, climb steeply to Middlesmoor and the start of a long off-road section which runs almost back to Pateley. A steady climb leads to a steep and rocky descent to Scar House Reservoir. There's barely time to catch your breath before the next rollercoaster tests your skills, climbing then dropping into and out of the steep gully formed by Woo Gill and Twizling Gill. The trail maintains its height above the patchwork of fields below before a gentle descent to Pot Moor High Road and a superb downhill, dropping 280m through the heather. There's a final climb just short of Wath. From here it's tarmac back to base.

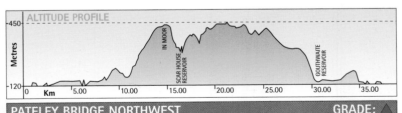

ALTITUDE PROFILE

Metres — 450 / 120

Km: 0, 5.00, 10.00, 15.00, 20.00, 25.00, 30.00, 35.00

IN MOOR — SCAR HOUSE RESERVOIR — GOUTHWAITE RESERVOIR

PATELEY BRIDGE NORTHWEST   GRADE: ▲

DISTANCE: 38KM

TOTAL ASCENT: 995M

START/FINISH: PATELEY BRIDGE

GRID REFERENCE: 157 654

PARKING: PAY & DISPLAY IN PATELEY BRIDGE

PUBLIC HOUSE: YORKE ARMS, RAMSGILL Tel: 01423 755243. CROWN HOTEL, MIDDLESMOOR Tel: 01423 755204. SPORTSMANS ARMS, WATH Tel: 01423 711306)

CAFÉ: LOTS OF CHOICE IN PATELEY BRIDGE. DOVENOR HOUSE, MIDDLESMOOR Tel: 01423 755697

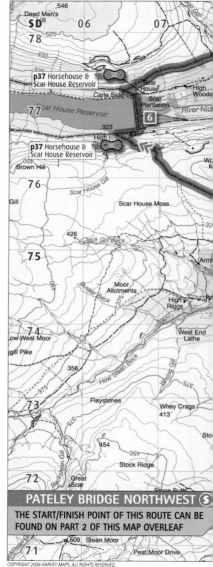

PATELEY BRIDGE NORTHWEST (S)

THE START/FINISH POINT OF THIS ROUTE CAN BE
FOUND ON PART 2 OF THIS MAP OVERLEAF

Pateley Bridge northwest (Part 1)

continues on NEXT PAGE

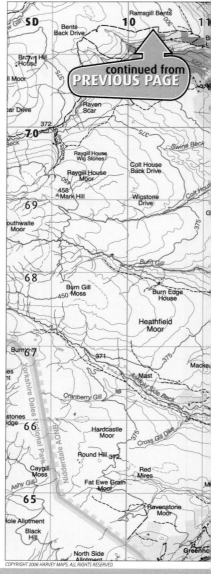

continued from
PREVIOUS PAGE

SD

10   11

Ramsgill Bents

Bents
Back Drive

Br..n Hill
House

..l Moor

.ar Drive

Raven
Scar

372

70

.eck

Swine Beck

Raygill House
Wig Stones

Raygill House
Moor

Colt House
Back Drive

458
Mark Hill

Wigstone
Drive

69

.outhwaite
Moor

Burn Gill

68

Burn Gill
450   Moss

Burn Edge
House

Heathfield
Moor

Burn .7   371

Mast

Macke.

Yorkshire Dales National Park

Cranberry Gill

Ashfold Side Beck

.stones
.idge   66

Hardcastle
Moor

Cross Gill Dike

Round Hill 372

Nidderdale AONB

Caygill
Moss

Fat Ewe Grain
Moor

Red
Mires

M.

Ashy Gill

65

Ravenstone
Moor

.ole Allotment

Black
Hill

North Side
Allotment

Greenho.

**Pateley Bridge
northwest (Part 2)**

Directions – Pateley Bridge northwest

→ From Pateley Bridge briefly follow the B6265 towards Grassington, cross the bridge over the River Nidd and soon turn first **R** onto Low Wath Road signposted *Ramsgill, Upper Nidderdale*.

2 Follow the road for almost 8km to the end of Gouthwaite Reservoir. Go past the Yorke Inn in Ramsgill and immediately after crossing a small bridge turn **L** onto a track aiming towards the *Bridleway to Stean* signpost. After almost 1km, as the broad stone and grass track turns sharp left uphill towards Grindstone Hill House continue **SA** alongside the wall on a grassy track which soon has a stone base.

3 A short steep rough climb leads up to then through West House Farm. Continue in the same direction following *Nidderdale Way* signposts. At the T-junction of tracks (GR 098 731) by a 3-way signpost and buildings turn **R** downhill signposted *Bridleway to Stean*.

4 Descend on cobbles. Go through Studfold Farm onto tarmac past a caravan park and take the first road to the **R** to cross a stone bridge over How Stean Beck. Shortly at the T-junction with a broader road turn **L** signposted *Middlesmoor only*.

5 Climb steeply through the village of Middlesmoor with its highly visible church and the Crown Hotel. Shortly after the tarmac turns to track **ignore** a broad stone track to the right then a *Private Road* to the left. Continue climbing for 2.5km.

6 The dam and reservoir come into sight and the track turns to rubble and loose stone on the descent. Join tarmac, turn **R** then **L** over the bridge. At the end of the dam bear **L** uphill on broad 'cobbled' track (in other words, **not** sharp left alongside the water). Shortly turn first **R**.

7 Climb then descend into a deep gully formed by Woo Gill and Twizling Gill (GR 079 778). Climb steeply. **Easy to miss:** shortly after the gradient eases, with a small stone building about 300m ahead turn **L** uphill towards the mining spoil heap then bear **R** after the heap through the gate and onto a better track.

8 The surface keeps improving. Continue in the same direction on the main track for 5km, ignoring turns to left and right, passing a stone shooting lodge with a green corrugated roof. At the road turn **L** then **R**. Shortly, at the fork of tracks about 200m after a gate at the top of the hill bear **R** gently downhill on the grassier track alongside the wall.

9 Long fine descent between walls. Cross a stone bridge over Lul Beck, climb, go through a gate (GR 136 727) and turn **R** towards a conifer plantation. At the T-junction of stone tracks beyond the woodland turn **R** to continue downhill signposted *Unsuitable for motors*.

10 Good descent. At the junction with tarmac turn **L** signposted *Bridleway to Wath*. The tarmac turns to track at Covill House Farm. After 800m at a fork of tracks stay on the lower right-hand one, closer to the water.

11 Final climb as the track bears away from the reservoir. At the T-junction (GR 148 681) just after a big house and barns turn **R** downhill.

12 At the T-junction with tarmac turn **R** towards the telephone box then at the next T-junction (after the Sportsmans Arms Hotel in Wath) turn **L** to join the outward route for 3.5 km back to Pateley Bridge.

◀◉◉ Making a day of it

Another ride starts from *Pateley Bridge*, heading west to Appletreewick – *see page 117*. Alternatively, link to the *Kirkby Malzeard* ride – *see page 85* – as they both use the track over Fountains Earth Moor. A third option would be to continue past *Scar House Reservoir* to the pub at Horsehouse then return the same way – *see page 37*.

Ribblehead, Dentdale & Great Knoutberry Hill

31.5km

Introduction

This ride has **variety!** From the iconic Ribblehead Viaduct and easy tracks by the railway, to the testing climb up the northeast flank of Whernside and on to the grassy plateau over Great Wold. Like rock gardens? Try the 6km long, 350m descent into Dentdale. Good on road climbs? Test yourself on the savage blast up from Dentdale to Dent Station. Lots of gears left in reserve? Didn't think so. Off-road again beyond the station, the Yorkshire Dales National Park Authority has made superb improvements to the once unrideable tracks around Great Knoutberry Hill and down Arten Gill, now a cobbled masterpiece with hop-across drainage channels in what was a totally washed-out boulder gully.

The Ride

An easy stone track leads under the famous Ribblehead viaduct and onto a long bridleway that climbs up and over Whernside to drop into Dentdale. This crosses every imaginable surface, from smooth gravel to loose rubble, pristine grass to stream beds and short muddy sections. Rattle down into Dentdale and turn left for coffee and buns or right for one of the toughest road climbs in the Dales, the infamous Coal Road up to Dent Station. The reward is a fantastic track contouring around Great Knoutberry and a sweeping descent dropping 250m down Arten Gill on a new path leading below the viaduct. More road climbing and an easy grassy bridleway lead back to Ribblehead.

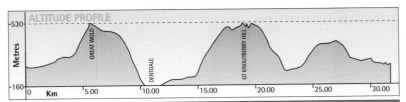

ALTITUDE PROFILE

Metres

GREAT WOLD

DENTDALE

GT KNOUTBERRY HILL

530						
160						
0	Km	5.00	10.00	15.00	20.00	25.00	30.00

RIBBLEHEAD, DENTDALE & GREAT KNOUTBERRY HILL   GRADE: ▲

DISTANCE: 31.5KM   **TOTAL ASCENT:** 990M

START/FINISH: CAR PARK BY RIBBLEHEAD VIADUCT ON THE B6255 BETWEEN HAWES AND INGLETON

PARKING: AS ABOVE   **GRID REFERENCE:** 764 792

PUBLIC HOUSE: STATION INN AT RIBBLEHEAD Tel: 015 242 41274   **CAFÉ:** LOTS OF CHOICE JUST OFF THE ROUTE IN DENT

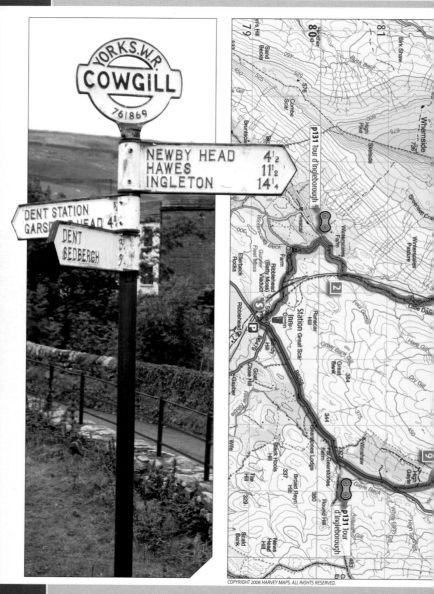

Ribblehead, Dentdale & Great Knoutberry Hill

Directions – Ribblehead, Dentdale & Great Knoutberry Hill

➎ From the car park just off the B6255 by the Station Inn at Ribblehead follow the broad stone track underneath the famous Ribblehead Viaduct. Continue on this track, keeping the Gunnerfleet Farm buildings to the right, cross a small bridge with a metal railing then at tarmac turn **R**. After a short climb, at the T-junction turn **R** signposted *Deepdale* to cross the cattlegrid.

2 Pass beneath the railway and turn **L** signposted *Bridleway to Dent*. The track starts off with an improved surface but there are short steep rough sections either side of the next bridge over the railway (by a small waterfall).

3 After the footpath to Whernside bears off left (GR 757 824) there is a very rough section. The better surface of smooth grass and stone at the summit (shown on the map as *Boot of the Wold*!) is followed by a new improved section of yellow/brown gravel.

4 The descent is at times rough and washed out but there are big views of Dentdale as compensation. At the lane turn **R** then shortly at the next T-junction turn **R** again (there is a house to the left).

5 Follow this lane eastwards up the valley for almost 4km. At the T-junction after the bridge over the River Dee turn **R** (no sign). After 500m turn **L** signposted *Dent Station* (or for a short cut missing out the Great Knoutberry Hill loop, continue **SA** signposted *Newby Head, Hawes* and rejoin at **8**).

6 Tough climb. The very steep gradient eases after Dent Station. About 650m after the end of the forestry (Dodderham Moss) on the left turn sharp **R** onto a broad stone track, climbing gently, to go through a gate (GR 779 881). Follow this recently improved balcony path for 2.6km.

7 At the T-junction of tracks by an Arten Gill information board turn **R** downhill for a fast descent (watch our for walkers). Pass beneath the viaduct. At the tarmac continue downhill then at the road junction by the bridge turn **L**.

8 Steep climb on road with the stream to the right. **Easy to miss:** after 3km and about 400m **after** the end of the forest (Mossy Bottom) on the right and 100m **before** a corrugated iron shack bear **R** through a bridlegate onto a grassy track signposted *Bridleway to the B6255* (GR 786 836).

9 The next 2km is generally rideable on grass or grass and stone trail. **Easy to miss:** shortly after passing a footpath signpost for *Gearstones* to the right, on a sharp right-hand bend with trees and Ingleborough in sight bear **L** (in effect **SA**) onto a grassy track through a gate (GR 788 817). Descend to join tarmac (the drive to High Gayle Farm) and bear **L**. At the B6255 turn **R** and follow for 3.5km back to the start.

←⬤⬤ Making a day of it

The *Tour d'Ingleborough* passes through Ribblehead – *see page 131*. If you turn left when you reach Dentdale you can link to the *Sedbergh* rides in this book's companion guide: *Yorkshire Dales Mountain Biking – The North Dales*.

SECTION 4

Killers

Character building...

We wouldn't go so far as to say that these loops could kill you, but they won't be much fun if you're not prepared.

Hard climbs, hard descents and plenty of 'em.

Killers
sponsored by

MALHAM TARN

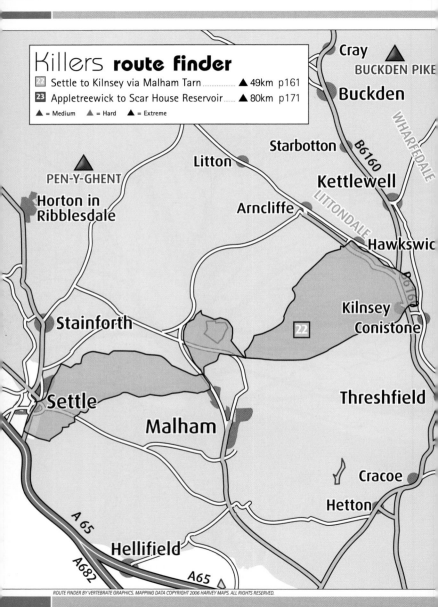

Killers **route finder**

22 Settle to Kilnsey via Malham Tarn .... ▲ 49km p161

23 Appletreewick to Scar House Reservoir ...... ▲ 80km p171

▲ = Medium   ▲ = Hard   ▲ = Extreme

Cray

BUCKDEN PIKE

Buckden

WHARFEDALE

Starbotton   B6160

Litton

Kettlewell

PEN-Y-GHENT

Horton in
Ribblesdale

Arncliffe

LITTONDALE

Hawkswic

Stainforth

B6160

Kilnsey

Conistone

Threshfield

Settle

Malham

Cracoe

Hetton

A 65

Hellifield

A682

A65

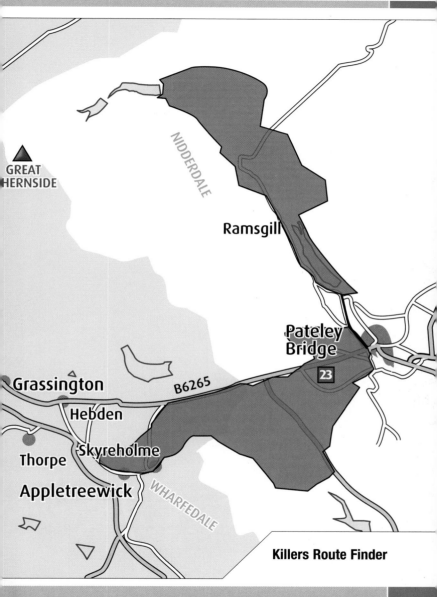

GREAT
HERNSIDE

NIDDERDALE

Ramsgill

Pateley
Bridge

23

Grassington

Hebden

B6265

Skyreholme

Thorpe

Appletreewick

WHARFEDALE

Killers Route Finder

"STAY ON THE ROAD. KEEP CLEAR OF THE MOORS." "BEWARE THE MOON, LADS!"

Settle to Kilnsey via Malham Tarn   49km

Introduction

Crossing from Ribblesdale to Wharfedale this ride links three classic routes in the National Park: *Mastiles Lane from Street Gate to Kilnsey*; *Arncliffe Cote to Malham Tarn*; and *Gorbeck Road from above Malham to Langcliffe*, each of which requires minimal route finding as soon as you find yourself pointed in the right direction. The ride passes through some of the finest scenery in the park beneath limestone cliffs at Settle Scar, above Malham Cove, around the superbly located Malham Tarn, along the old drovers' road of Mastiles Lane, beneath Kilnsey Crag, returning via Old Cote Moor Top. At each stage there are tough climbs, high-level cruising and descents to dream of, particularly down towards Malham Cove, down to Kilnsey then the final teeth-rattler to return to Settle.

The Ride

Heading south from Settle, swing east off-road, climbing to Stockdale Farm. The rocky summit leads on to a grassy descent with the stunning backdrop of Malham Cove. Lanes take you over the plateau to an easy cruise through woodland around the shores of Malham Tarn. An undulating ride along Mastiles Lane reaches the route's 423m highpoint before dropping swiftly to Kilnsey and a chance to refuel for your summit attempt on High Cote Moor. Enjoy the grassy descent and the long stony stream bed crossing before rejoining tarmac at Street Gate. A cut through from Water Sinks leads almost directly to Gorbeck Road, a long stretch of improved path that seems to float above the soft moorland either side. Final fireworks come with the 150m downhill from the Langcliffe road into the very heart of Settle. Phew!

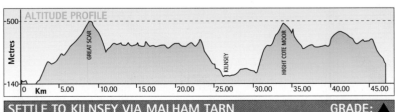

ALTITUDE PROFILE

Metres

GREAT SCAR KILNSEY HIGHT COTE MOOR

| Km | 5.00 | 10.00 | 15.00 | 20.00 | 25.00 | 30.00 | 35.00 | 40.00 | 45.00 |

SETTLE TO KILNSEY VIA MALHAM TARN   GRADE: ▲

DISTANCE: 49KM

START/FINISH: SETTLE

PARKING: LOTS OF PAY & DISPLAY CAR PARKS IN SETTLE

PUBLIC HOUSE: TENNANT ARMS, KILNSEY Tel: 01756 752301

TOTAL ASCENT: 1330M

GRID REFERENCE: 820 636

CAFÉ: LOTS OF CHOICE IN SETTLE

Settle to Kilnsey via Malham Tarn (Part 1)

continued from **PREVIOUS PAGE**

Settle to Kilnsey via Malham Tarn (Part 2)

Directions – Settle to Kilnsey
via Malham Tarn

⑤ Follow the B6480 south from the centre of Settle towards the railway station and Skipton. Go past the Falcon Manor Hotel then 800m after passing under the railway bridge turn **L** onto a broad stone track immediately before a low stone house and opposite a tall wooden *Settle town* sign (GR 813623).

2 Cross a bridge over the railway and climb steadily. Go through Lodge Farm, turn **L** then shortly at a fork bear **R** uphill between stone walls. Views back down to Settle. Keep climbing on 'cobble effect' trail. At a T-junction with a major stone track (GR 828 624) turn **L** gently downhill then shortly turn first **R** sharply back on yourself signposted *Bridleway, Settle Loop*.

3 At the T-junction with the road turn **R** then take the first lane to the **L** signposted *Bridleway* and follow tarmac for 2.3km. At a fork of tracks at the end of the tarmac lane (with Stockdale Farm down to the right), bear **L** through a gate onto a narrower stone track alongside the wall.

4 The stone track turns to grass then becomes rocky for the summit before turning back to grass. Go through a gate with tall slate slabs as supports. Continue towards Cove Road, **ignoring** a bridleway to the left to *Langscar Gate*. Long descent on grass then grass and stone. Go through the gate and turn **L** uphill on the road.

5 At the X-roads after 3km go **SA** signposted *Arncliffe*. At the T-junction bear **R** also signposted *Arncliffe*. After 800m, and soon after the start of the trees on the right turn **R** on a tarmac lane by a *Malham Tarn National Trust* signpost. Pass around the back of the Field Centre to continue in the same direction.

6 Stay on the main stone track close the tarn. Go through a gate in a wall and follow the stone track as it bears **L** away from the tarn (there is a *Pennine Way, Water Sinks Gate* sign pointing right onto a grassy track). After 800m, at the road turn **L** towards a gate in the wall.

7 Go through the gate signposted *No cars or motorbikes, Kilnsey 5 miles* onto the track running alongside the wall on the right. After 700m descend to cross Gordale Beck via the ford or clapper bridge. Climb and continue along the undulating main track on a variety of surfaces (parts are likely to be muddy in winter). Go through a gate onto an enclosed track with walls to right and left, ignoring turnings off to the right.

8 The track climbs to the third and final summit (423m) about 5km after leaving tarmac and the track improves from grass & stone to a fine, firm, stone-based track. Great descent over 2.5km. Join tarmac and bear **R**.

9 Descend to the B6160 by the Tennant Arms in Kilnsey and turn **L**. Go past the overhanging rocks at Kilnsey Crag and after 1km take the first road to the **L** signposted *Arncliffe, Litton*.

10 After a further 3km go past Hawkswick Caravan Park, round a sharp right-hand bend then turn **L** onto a tarmac lane signposted *Arncliffe Cote, Bridleway to Street Gate*. Continue **SA** at the end of tarmac through a gate onto a steep and stony track. At the second gate follow the main grassy track round to the **R** alongside the wall, zig-zagging up the hillside. You soon come to a grassy fork – take either track as they both rejoin. The generally excellent grassy track splits on a few occasions but all options lead up to the highpoint which is roughly halfway between Arncliffe Cote and Street Gate (4km after leaving the road).

11 On the descent you will need to go through a shallow stream bed/ford but it is stone-based and rideable. Descend through a final gate and on to tarmac. Continue **SA** for 100m then at the junction with the road bear **R** signposted *Settle*.

12 After 1km, go past a car parking area on the right, cross a stream then turn **L** through a gate onto a grass track signposted *Bridleway to Langscar Gate*. Shortly bear **R** uphill at a fork by a *Langscar Gate* signpost.

13 At the road turn **L** to cross the cattle grid and turn immediately **R** through a gate, uphill onto a grassy track. After 300m at a fork of grassy tracks bear **R** alongside the wall. Soon join a superb new stone track for the next 6km (with one short unimproved section). Great views to the right to Pen-y-ghent and Ingleborough.

14 Descend. At the road turn **L** and immediately **L** again through a gate onto a track signposted *Bridleway to Settle*. Mainly grassy descent through gates then a steep stone downhill. Join the road, turn **L** to descend down to the square in the centre of Settle.

PASSING MINING RUINS

Appletreewick to Scar House Reservoir

80km

Introduction

This is the longest ride here with the most climbing. However, it contains a fine mix of farm tracks, rocky gullies and wide open grouse moor, almost all rideable and fast enough to mean you don't need to be an Olympic medallist to do this in a (long) day. As 'enjoyable' climbs go, the one from Appletreewick onto Pock Stones Moor ranks highly for scenery and challenge. A fine moor track leads to Pateley, which is full of cafés, so you won't be stuck for carbs. Roads lead north up Nidderdale and an almost entirely off-road run then returns to Wath. The final section explores lead mining ruins, climbing on to Craven Moor before the final descent, right into Appletreewick.

The Ride

Tarmac then good stone tracks lead from the pretty village of Appletreewick up onto the moor. Rejoin tarmac, cross the River Washburn and face the worst part of the ride – 1km of unsigned reedy plodding over Braithwaite Moor to join a much better grouse moor track dropping towards Pateley. Climb the west side of the Nidd Valley on tarmac and a stone track onto In Moor. A rock and rubble descent to Scar House Reservoir crosses the rough gully formed by Woo Gill and Twizling Gill (great names!). Then swing down the east side of the valley on a long, high, cruise to a fast descent to Bouthwaite. Ride alongside Gouthwaite Reservoir to Wath, turning west to a climb through mining ruins, a sprint along the road and a fine downhill to complete the ride.

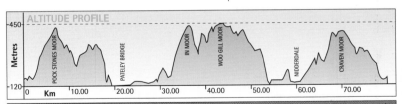

ALTITUDE PROFILE

POCK STONES MOOR · PATELEY BRIDGE · IN MOOR · WOO GILL MOOR · NIDDERDALE · CRAVEN MOOR

Metres: -450 to -120

Km: 0 · 10.00 · 20.00 · 30.00 · 40.00 · 50.00 · 60.00 · 70.00

APPLETREEWICK TO SCAR HOUSE RESERVOIR   GRADE: ▲

DISTANCE: 80KM

START/FINISH: NEW INN, APPLETREEWICK

PARKING: AT THE NEW INN

TOTAL ASCENT: 1470M

GRID REFERENCE: 054 601

CAFÉ: LOTS OF CHOICE IN PATELEY BRIDGE

PUBLIC HOUSE: LOTS OF CHOICE IN PATELEY BRIDGE. YORKE ARMS RAMSGILL Tel: 01423 755243.
CROWN HOTEL, MIDDLESMOOR Tel: 01423 755204. SPORTSMANS ARMS, WATH Tel: 01423 711306

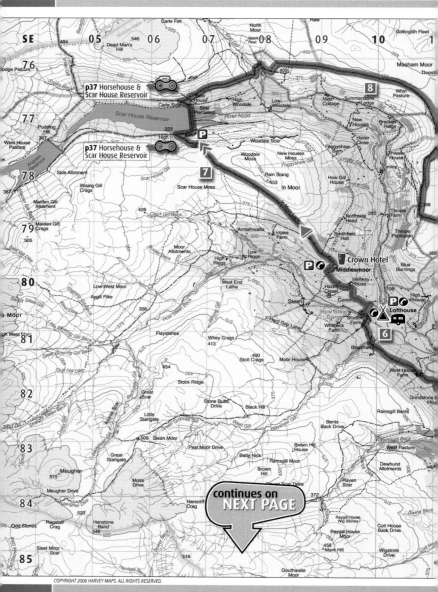

continues on
NEXT PAGE

Appletreewick to Scar House Reservoir (Part 1)

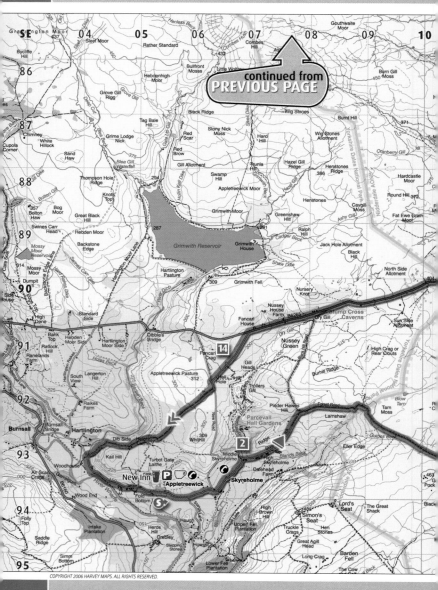

continued from
PREVIOUS PAGE

Appletreewick to Scar House Reservoir (Part 2)

Directions – Appletreewick to Scar House Reservoir

⤵ From the New Inn in Appletreewick head east following signs for *Skyreholme and Pateley Bridge*. **Ignore** a right turn signposted *Skipton, Bolton Abbey*. Climb and take the next **R** onto a no through road signposted *Skyreholme*. At the T-junction (with Parcevall Hall to the left) turn **R** to cross the bridge.

2 Steady climb to the end of tarmac. At the junction of tracks (GR 078 616) as the left-hand track swings sharply uphill bear **R** signposted *No cars or motor bikes except for access*. Superb climb on excellent quality track. Descend from the summit to cross Harden Gill, short climb then longer descent. At the road turn **L** downhill. Once again down then up, crossing River Washburn. At the T-junction at the end of Hoodstorth Lane turn **L** signposted *Pateley Bridge*.

3 After 1km go past Humberstone Bank on the left then shortly turn **R** through a gate towards High House Farm signposted *Bridleway*. Pass to the **L** of buildings, go through two gates and alongside the wall on the **right-hand** edge of the field. The next kilometre is rough: go through the next gate (with Palleys Crags ahead) and turn **L** alongside wall on a barely visible track through reedy grass, following the occasional wooden post. Join a more distinct path by a signpost (blue arrows/yellow background) and turn **R** alongside the wall.

4 Join an excellent stone-based track leading through heather towards Pateley Bridge. Keep bearing **L** on an ever better track to descend to the road and turn **R** downhill. Follow the steep, dark lane through woodland. At the T-junction at the end of Peat Lane turn **L** downhill. Bear **R** at a fork of lanes down a hill signposted *1 in 7*. At the T-junction in Pateley turn **R** then after 150m turn **L** onto Low Wath Road signposted *Ramsgill, Upper Nidderdale*.

5 Follow the road for almost 8km to the end of Gouthwaite Reservoir. Go past the Yorke Inn in Ramsgill and immediately after a small bridge turn **L** onto track aiming towards the *Bridleway to Stean* signpost. After almost 1km, as the stone and grass track turns sharp left uphill towards Grindstone Hill House continue **SA** alongside the wall on a grassy track which soon has a stone base. A short steep rough climb leads up to then through West House Farm. Continue in the same direction following *Nidderdale Way* signposts. At the T-junction of tracks (GR 098 731) by a 3-way signpost and buildings turn **R** downhill signposted *Bridleway to Stean*.

6   Descend through Studfold Farm onto tarmac past a caravan park and take the first road to the **R** to cross a stone bridge over How Stean Beck. Shortly at the T-junction with a broader road turn **L** signposted *Middlesmoor only*. Climb steeply through the village of Middlesmoor. Shortly after the tarmac turns to track ignore a broad stone track to the right then a Private Road to the left. Continue climbing.

7   The reservoir comes into sight and the track turns to loose stone on the descent. Join tarmac, turn **R** then **L** over the bridge. At the end of the dam bear **L** uphill on broad 'cobbled' track (**not** alongside water, in other words). Shortly turn first **R**. Climb then descend into deep gully formed by Woo Gill and Twizling Gill (GR 079 778). Climb steeply. **Easy to miss:** shortly after the gradient eases, with a small stone building about 300m ahead turn **L** uphill towards the mining spoil heap then bear **R** after the heap through the gate and onto a better track.

8   The track keeps improving. Continue in the same direction on the main track, **ignoring** turns to left and right, passing a stone shooting lodge with a green corrugated roof. At the road turn **L** then **R**. Shortly, at the fork of tracks about 200m after a gate at the top of the climb bear **R** gently downhill on the grassier track alongside the wall. Long fine descent between walls. Cross a stone bridge over Lul Beck, climb, go through a gate (GR 136 727) and turn **R** towards a conifer plantation.

9   At the T-junction of stone tracks beyond the woodland turn **R** to continue downhill signposted *Unsuitable for motors*. At the junction with tarmac turn **L** signposted *Bridleway to Wath*. The tarmac turns to track at Covill House. After 800m at a fork of tracks stay on the lower right-hand one, closer to the water. At the T-junction (GR 148 681) turn **R** downhill (just after a big house and barns).

10   At the T-junction with tarmac turn **R** towards the telephone box then at the next T-junction (after the Sportsmans Arms Hotel in Wath) turn **L** to join the outward route for 1.5 km towards Pateley Bridge. Take the first road to the **R** signposted *Heathfield* then shortly turn **L** signposted *Heathfield Caravan Park, Bridleway*. Go through several caravan sites following the main tarmac road, keeping **L** at forks.

11   At the end of the tarmac follow the good stone track alongside the stream and through broadleaf woodland. Shortly after going through two closely spaced gates, with a Private Road ahead, bear **L** downhill off the main track signposted *Nidderdale Way*. Cross the river and zig-zag up the hillside through ruins and spoil heaps (a bit confusing – there are several tracks), fairly soon joining a good broad gravel and grass track going straight up the hillside, passing to the **R** of a summit of outcrops of stones.

12   At a 3-way signpost continue **SA** downhill signposted *Bridleway to Pateley Bridge & Toft Gate*. Keep following *Nidderdale Way* signs down to cross the stream then climb. At the T-junction with the road turn **L** by a *Roundhill Farm* sign (GR 131 653) then shortly take the first **R** sharply back on yourself on a tarmac and grass lane signposted *Toft Gate*. **Easy to miss:** after 200m and immediately **before** the cattlegrid bear **R** away from the stone track onto a grassy track towards a gate with a white sign on it.

13   At the T-junction with tarmac turn **L** to continue uphill then shortly at the T-junction with the B6265 turn **R**. Descend, climb, descend, passing the Miners Arms, a church, a mast and Stump Cross Caverns. After 5.5km, shortly after the start of a climb, take the first road to the **L** signposted *Appletreewick*.

14   After 1.2km and soon after a sharp left-hand bend turn **R** through a gate signposted *Bridleway to Hartington*. At the fork of tracks after 1.4km bear **R** to go through a gate onto a walled track (the left fork goes down to a barn). At the road turn **L** to return to Appletreewick.

◄◯◯ Making a day of it

You're kidding, right?

SECTION 5

Bonus Section

Gisburn Forest –
*waymarked trails and lots of potential
just outside the Park boundaries.*

Top ten climbs –
*clean them all, no dabs,
and you've earned yourself a cake.*

Top ten descents –
reward enough in themselves!

Top ten cruises –
*enjoy the view,
the feel of the wind in your hair...*

Bonus Section
sponsored by

www.polaris apparel.co.uk

Red Route

through **GISBURN FOREST**

Introduction

There is no Forestry Commission land in the National Park, so there's no man-made singletrack. The nearest is here at Gisburn or to the north at Hamsterley. Here in Gisburn there are three way-marked routes, all pretty straightforward with only a couple of tricky climbs – they make great rides for novices or partners who venture out only occasionally. But dig a little deeper, and you'll notice signs of more interesting trails hidden in the woodland (including old XC and DH race courses). It's an area where local knowledge is vital as it would be impossible to describe them in detail. If you want to find them it's a case of making a few trips and getting lost a few times. You'll probably find it's well worth while!

The Ride

From the route signboard in the car park, the waymarked trails (red, green and purple) overlap at the start. After an isolated barn there are some slightly overgrown single-track sections. At one point you emerge at the road to cross the bridge over Stocks Reservoir then dive back into woodland. Keep an eye out for the waymarks – they can become obscured by vegetation. After a lot of easy riding you are suddenly faced with two short steep climbs with roots across the path to add to the fun. If you need somewhere to stop and eat, there are picnic tables inside and outside a second barn (Martin's Laithe Shelter). Two stream crossings also may present a challenge if water levels are high. The ride has been largely up on the way out, so it's downhill for most of the return.

THE RED ROUTE THROUGH GISBURN FOREST   GRADE: ▲

DISTANCE: 16KM   **TOTAL ASCENT:** 170M

START/FINISH: COCKLET HILL CAR PARK, WELL SIGNPOSTED OFF THE B6478 CLITHEROE –
LONG PRESTON ROAD, ABOUT 5KM NORTHEAST OF SLAIDBURN

PARKING: AS ABOVE   **GRID REFERENCE:** 746 550

CAFÉ: NONE. NEAREST IS IN SLAIDBURN   **PUBLIC HOUSE:** NONE. NEAREST IS IN SLAIDBURN

↪ Start from Cocklet Hill car park. From the Gisburn Forest bike route signboard follow the red arrows (for much of the route it shares the same course as the green route and for a good part the purple route as well).

2 The first 500m is repeated on the outward and return route. About 1.5km after the start you briefly join the road to cross the causeway over Stocks Reservoir before diving back into woodland.

3 The route is in general very well signposted and it is impossible to give comprehensive instructions through woodland without referring to the bike route waymarking. There are a couple of short very steep climbs, some singletrack and a couple of stream crossings. The route is generally climbing for the first half of the ride and descending for the second half.

RACE YA!

Rubble, slippery limestone, steep slopes, steep slopes, streaming eyes...
This isn't even really a 'top' ten – such a small number of descents wouldn't do the Dales justice! If you want more, try the drop into Litton from Haw Fell; to Scar House from In Moor or into Bolton Abbey from Halton Moor...

North of Clapham (Clapham and Feizor)   GR 764721

South from Long Scar on smooth grass just spot-on for skips and jumps to a full-on stony enclosed track leading down through the famous tunnels to Clapham.

Halton Gill from Horsehead (Horton, Horse Head and Foxup)   GR 889776

A 300m descent of pure adrenaline with quintessential Dales scenery spread out like a tablecloth below.

Stainforth (Stainforth and Littondale)   GR 834660

Only 150m of descent but a great blast to finish off this long ride.

Kettlewell or Starbotton from Old Cote Moor Top
(Buckden and LIttondale)   GR 951735

An innocuous grassy start leads to a rubble-fest, then, just when you thought it was all over, a slippery washed-out section. Alternately, descend from the same point to Starbotton – narrow, rocky and slippery with a big drop to the right. Not for the faint of heart or unsure of steering! 300m descent.

Starbotton (Kettlewell Circuit)   GR 970753

Precipitous 300m descent from Cam Head on a mixture of all you'd ever want in a Yorkshire Dales downhill.

Settle (Settle, Malham and Gorbeck)   GR 838655

Starting from the west end of the improved Gorbeck track drop 250m down into the heart of Settle on an ever steeper trail to emerge blinking in the bright lights.

Arncliffe Cote (Kilnsey and Mastiles Lane)   GR 925685

A long grassy monster, non-stop fun on this 300m descent into Littondale.

Weets Top (Gargrave and Grassington Circuits)   GR 925632

Two for the price of one – newly improved tracks from Weets Top let you glide southwest down to Calton or southeast to Hetton – 220m drop in each case.

Arkleside Moor (Horsehouse and Scar House Reservoir)   GR 044782

A tale of two descents – Horsehouse to Scar House Reservoir is a there-and-back track with a challenging rocky 150m drop from the highpoint down to the reservoir or a longer faster blast dropping 230m from the same highpoint on your way back to Horsehouse.

Mastiles Lane to Kilnsey (Killer Loop 1)   GR 950665

See it all ahead of you from the final summit on Mastiles Lane down the walled stone-based beauty into Wharfedale.

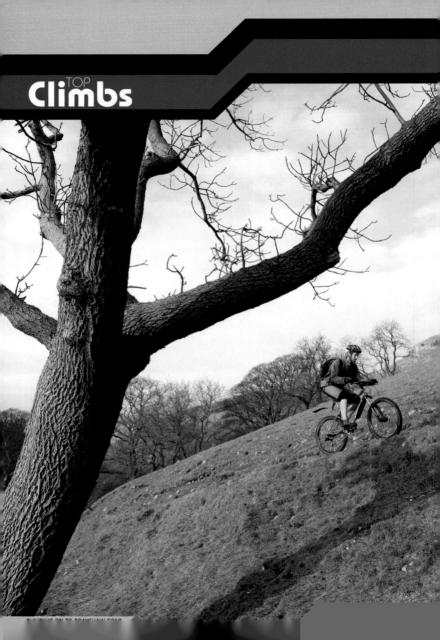

Always a difficult one to choose!

The best climbs are not the steepest and roughest as these are pushes (no one could ride from Raisgill in Langstrothdale up to Horse Head...) but steep enough and testing enough to feel a sense of achievement if you manage them without a dab. Surface conditions can change, making a trail that is just rideable on a dry summer's day a complete no-no in the depths of winter. Here is a selection which you can take as you will:

Clapham to Selside (Clapham and Feizor)   GR 746694

Up through the tunnels near Clapham, a short respite then on up to Long Scar.

Pennine Way north of Horton
(Horton, Horse Head and Foxup)   GR 808727

Steady 150m climb, most likely watched by Pennine Way walkers so you can't get off!

Arncliffe Cote (Stainforth and Littondale & Killer 1)   GR 818697

One of the few well-drained grassy challenges – 300m up from Littondale towards Malham.

Kettlewell (Kettlewell Circuit)   GR 972724

All the way, No dabs. Steep tarmac then loose stone – and nowhere to recover – on the first half. Flatter, but stickier and with some slippery bits on the upper section.

South of Settle (Settle, Malham and Gorbeck)   GR 813623

It's 350m up from the B6480 south of Settle to Kirkby Fell on your way to Malham. Easy – hard – easy – hard. The top!

Kilnsey (Kilnsey and Mastiles Lane)   GR 973678

Mastiles Lane heading west from Kilnsey – touch and go if riding into a strong westerly wind (250m climb).

Calton to Weets Top (Gargrave and Mastiles Lane)   GR 909593

Just when you thought it would get harder as you got higher, the National Park has created a splendid track taking you right up to Weets Top (220m climb).

East of Appletreewick (Pateley Bridge and Appletreewick)   GR 077614

Very fine stone surface on this 220m climb across the heather moor up to Great Pock Stones.

In Moor from Middlesmoor (Pateley Bridge & Scar House Res.)   GR 092742

Only 130m climb off-road but just rough enough to test skills and stamina.

Horsehouse climb (Horsehouse & Scar House Res.)   GR 044804

This is one where every drop of sweat expended getting to the top is rewarded by a descent on the same track on the way back (240m climb).

CRUISING NEAR APPLETREEWICK

The best *specialités de la région* of the Dales are the well-drained grassy summits and the broad grouse moor tracks offering top grade traverses. Admire the view and cruise!

North of Clapham (Tour d'Ingleborough)   GR 767720–787746

Ogle at the great slabs of limestone pavement as you cruise through Three Peaks country on firm grassy tracks with a gentle 100m drop down into upper Ribblesdale.

Dawson Close west of Litton, off the Stainforth–Halton Gill road
(Stainforth & Littondale)   GR 856728–898742

Leave the Stainforth–Halton Gill road and a gentle climb on a manicured stone track leads to an easy, gliding 160m descent diagonally across the hillside down into the delights of Littondale.

Gorbeck - Malham towards Langcliffe (Stainforth, Settle & Killer 1) GR 888649–830653

Magnificent work by the National Park has built an easy stone-based trail snaking across the moorland.

Mastiles Lane, the plateau section from Street Gate to Mastiles Gate
(Kilnsey and Mastiles Lane & Killer 1)   GR 905657–944662

Ancient walled track dating from Roman times used for droving sheep to and from Wharfedale. A mixture of all sorts of surfaces – be prepared for mud in winter. A mighty descent if you are heading east.

Barden Moor, west of Bolton Abbey
(Embsay & Bolton Abbey)   GR 037554–973578

A stone-based beauty through the heather with the Barden Reservoirs glittering in the sunshine.

East of Appletreewick, across Pock Stones Moor
(Pateley Bridge and Appletreewick & Killer 2)   GR 091695–128594

A gentle up and over at the top of a steep climb from Appletreewick through the heather.

Sype Land/Fountains Earth Moor above Nidderdale to the northeast of
Gouthwaite Reservoir (Pateley Bridge and Scar House Reservoir)   GR 135791–115750

One of several fine broad tracks through this great heather-clad plateau above Nidderdale at 300-400m.

Above Nidderdale to the east of Scar House Reservoir over North Moor & Pott Moor
(Pateley Bridge and Scar House Reservoir & Killer 2)   GR 083779–114750

Cruise along the edge of the valley past the shooting lodges with Nidderdale steeply below you.

Over Masham Moor/Grewelthorpe Moor west of Masham
(Masham and Masham Moor)   GR 141747–188780

The longest and best of the moor cruises. A series of undulations leads to a fast open 120m descent.

Along the Turbary Road above Kingsdale
(Ingleton Loop)   GR 700785–676764

A pleasant grassy run with views as far as Morecambe Bay if you're lucky. Better still are the underground rivers. Listen out for a couple of DEEP holes on the south side of the trail...

Appendices

Tourist Information Offices

Clapham	Tel: 015242 51419
Grassington	Tel: 01756 752774
	grassington@ytbtic.co.uk
High Bentham	Tel: 015242 62549
Horton in Ribblesdale	Tel: 01729 860333
	horton@ytbtic.co.uk
Ilkley	Tel: 01943 602319
	ilkley@ytbtic.co.uk
Ingleton	Tel: 015242 41049
	ingletontic@hotmail.com
Kirkby Lonsdale	Tel: 015242 71437
	kltic@southlakeland.gov.uk
Malham	Tel: 01729 830363
	malham@ytbtic.co.uk
Pateley Bridge	Tel: 01423 711147
	pateleybridge@ytbtic.co.uk
Ripon	Tel: 01765 604625
	ripontic@harrogate.gov.uk
Settle	Tel: 01729 825192
	settle@ytbtic.co.uk
Skipton	Tel: 01756 792809
	skipton@ytbtic.co.uk

Weather

www.bbc.co.uk/weather

www.metoffice.com

The Dales Bike Bus

The **Bike Bus** is a rather special feature of the Dales. It's a bus with a fancy trailer that will transport you and your bike from Leeds into the heart of the Dales. An information leaflet is available from National Park Centres.

Tel: 01756 752774 for more information.

Accommodation

Youth Hostels

Visit www.yha.org.uk

Dentdale	Tel: 0870 770 5790
Hawes	Tel: 0870 770 5854
Ingleton	Tel: 0870 770 5880
Kettlewell	Tel: 0870 770 5896
Malham	Tel: 0870 770 5946
Slaidburn	Tel: 0870 770 6034
Stainforth	Tel: 0870 770 6046

Hotels, Self Catering & B&B

Your best bet is to have a look on the websites listed later in this section, or to contact the Tourist Information Centre nearest to where you plan to ride.

Campsites

There are campsites dotted all over the area. There are at least two near Malham, and others near Horton, Ingleton and Kirkby Lonsdale.

Food and Drink

Cafés

There are hundreds of cafes around, so we're just going to list a couple of faves. See the individual rides for more.

Dalesman Café
Gargrave   Tel: 01756 749250

The Cove Centre
Malham   Tel: 01729 830432

Pen-y-Ghent Café
Horton in Ribbleside   Tel: 01729 860333

Pubs

Again, there are loads. See the individual rides for recommendations.

The New Inn
Appletreewick   Tel: 01756 720252

Buck Inn
Buckden   Tel: 01756 760228

Station Inn
Ribblehead   Tel: 015242 41274

Bike Shops

Hawes

Kudu Bikes
Also do bike hire   Tel: 01969 666088

Ingleton

Inglesports
Limited range of spares Tel: 015 242 41146

Kettlewell

Over and Under (Outdoor Clothing)
Limited range of spares Tel: 01756 760871

Pateley Bridge

Nidderdale Motors
Limited range of spares Tel: 01423 711309

Settle

The Station Yard   Tel: 01729 822216

There are loads more outside the National Park boundary:

Harrogate

Ace Cycles   Tel: 01423 508417

Boneshakers   Tel: 01423 709453

Cawthorn Cycles   Tel: 01423 888846

Cycle Way   Tel: 01423 566215

Psychlosport   Tel: 01423 545413

Ilkley

JD Cycles Shop
Also do bike hire   Tel: 01943 816101

Bike Shops (continued)

Kendal

Askew Cycles   Tel: 01539 728057

Brucie's Bikes   Tel: 01539 727230

Lancaster

The Edge Cycleworks   Tel: 01524 840800

Skipton

The Bicycle Shop   Tel: 01756 794386

Dave Ferguson Cycles
Also do bike hire   Tel: 01756 795367

Ripon

Moonglu   Tel: 01765 601106

Otley

Chevin Cycles   Tel: 01943 462773

Bike Hire

Forgotten to bring your bike?

Ingleton

Howsons
Main Street   Tel: 015 242 41422

Fremington

Dales Mountain Bike Hire
     Tel: 01748 884356

Other Websites/ Publications

www.yorkshiredales.org.uk

www.yorkshire-dales.com

www.mtbthedales.org.uk

Where to Mountain Bike in Britain
Nicky Crowther, Open Air Books

The Dales Bike Liveries

The Yorkshire Dales is well on the way to becoming the first national park in Britain to establish a system of Bike Liveries across its region. The plan is for fully equipped bike liveries to be located at various MTB-friendly pubs and cafés throughout the region and will offer riders secure bike storage, workshops, hoses and so on.

Modelled on John Pitcher's awesome facility behind the **New Inn** in Appletreewick, liveries will be established in key areas of the park, such as Settle, Hawes and Reeth.

Baggage handling will be offered between liveries, making point-to-point multi-day rides across the Dales a real option. Guiding services will also be available.

Contact the **YDNPA** or **John Pitchers** for more information.

The Author

Nick Cotton

Nick Cotton has written over 30 bike guides in the last 12 years, riding more than 20,000 miles all over Britain during the course of his research. He has travelled and trekked extensively, climbing to over 18,000ft on three continents and has cycled in Morocco and Patagonia (the worst winds in the world!).

He lives in the Lune Valley in Cumbria, between the Lakes and the Dales. He is very partial to fine coffee, real ale and cakes, especially on the course of a ride. Six feet four and 14 stones needs a lot of fuel.

The photographer

Andy Heading

Despite regular trips *oop north* over the years (mainly for Polaris and Trailquest events), Andy's lasting memory of the Dales was getting two 'volunteers' to dress up as Wallace and Gromit for a cheesy Wensleydale photo-feature. Since photographing this guide, he's realised there's much more to Yorkshire than cursing and were-rabbits, and looks forward to biking there again soon. In the meantime, he is the official photographer to the European Athletic Association, and lives in a cheese-free zone in Matlock, Derbyshire.

Vertebrate Graphics

Vertebrate Graphics Ltd is a full service graphic design agency, specialising in print design, web development and publishing. We design a wide range of communication material from wedding stationery to corporate brochures.

As well as being one of the largest agencies in the UK to work within the outdoor leisure sector, our experienced team of designers produce work for IT companies, educational organisations, including colleges and universities, financial institutions and the retail sector.

For more information please refer to our website at **www.v-graphics.co.uk**, or contact us direct at **info@v-graphics.co.uk**.

Vertebrate Graphics has had substantial success in the design and production of specialist outdoor books. These include **Hillwalking – The Official Handbook of the Mountain Leader and Walking Group Leader Schemes** (a best-selling outdoor title for three years running), and two highly praised guidebooks for rock climbers – the award-winning **Lake District Rock – Selected Rock Climbs in The Lake District** and **The Roaches – Staffordshire Grit**.

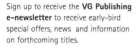

Order form for

Vertebrate Graphics

PUBLICATIONS & CD-ROMS

Item	Qty	Price
hill & trail **walking** » books		(inc P&P)
Day Walks in the Peak District		£12.95
mountain **biking** » books & cd-roms		
Yorks Dales – South MTB Book		£15.95
Yorks Dales – South CD-ROM		£7.50
Yorks Dales – South Book & CD-ROM Bundle		£21.00
White Peak MTB Book		£14.95
White Peak CD-ROM		£7.50
White Peak Book & CD-ROM Bundle		£20.00
Dark Peak MTB Book		£14.95
Dark Peak CD-ROM		£7.50
Dark Peak Book & CD-ROM Bundle		£20.00
South West MTB Book		£14.95
South West CD-ROM		£7.50
South West Book & CD-ROM Bundle		£20.00
other » books		
Getting to Grips with GPS		£14.95
TOTAL £		

Fill in this coupon and send it along with a cheque to:
Vertebrate Graphics,
Crescent House, 228 Psalter Lane, Sheffield S11 8UT
Make cheques payable to **Vertebrate Graphics Ltd**.
Credit card payments are accepted at our website. Orders dispatched by return.

Name: ....

Address: ....

....

Postcode: ....

E-mail: ....

☐ **Vertebrate Graphics** will never pass on your details to third parties, but if you do not want to receive information on future VG Hill Walking, Mountain Biking or Climbing and Bouldering Guides, please tick here.

You can also place your order @ www.**v-graphics**.co.uk/publications